AF508018

IN THE ZONE WITH YOUR CHILD

Rediscover the Joy of Learning
and Become the Grown-Up You Always Needed

Carmen Gamper

Illustrations by Sybille Kramer

Cover Image *Mind in Flow* by Carmen Gamper

ISBN: 979-8-9950507-4-2

Library of Congress Number: 2026909185

First Edition 2026

Gamper, Carmen Viktoria, 1976-, author. In the zone with your child : rediscover the joy of learning and become the grown-up you always needed / Carmen Viktoria Gamper. San Francisco, CA : New Learning Culture, 2026. | Includes bibliographical references.

LCSH: Child psychology. | Child development. | Child rearing. | Parent and child. | Attention. | BISAC: FAMILY & RELATIONSHIPS / Parenting / General. | PSYCHOLOGY / Developmental / Child. | EDUCATION / Parent Participation.

New Learning Culture Publishing
California • USA

To The Child In You

Contents

THE MIND IN FLOW

LOVE

Preface

The Unexpected Journey We All Signed Up For

For Grown-Ups and the Children Who Transform Us

Children shape us. They challenge us. Whether through joy or chaos, they call us to become more than we were yesterday. They move us out of our comfort zones. They slow us down, stretch our patience, and invite us to love more deeply than we ever thought we could.

And as children, we did the same. We stretched our parents, our teachers, our caregivers, often without even knowing it.

It takes a big heart to slow down enough to truly meet a child where they are. And it's not easy. On the contrary, it's like trying to find stillness while navigating whirlwinds of needs and emotions: a toddler reaching for your hand, a frustrated child caught in playground politics, or a brooding teenager suddenly asking if you believe in unconditional love.

But when we do, when we get down to the height of a child and tune in for a moment, something powerful happens. We open a door to connection, to transformation and to becoming. And whether we realize it or not, this process draws us into a healing journey that includes our own childhood too.

Most parents don't remember checking the box that said, "Yes, I'd like to relive my unresolved childhood while sleep-deprived and covered in applesauce." You just wanted a family, a warm home, a clean kitchen, joy and fun together. Then, this child comes along. A little wild card in pajamas, full of mystery, mischief, and radiant life.

Suddenly, nothing goes as planned and everything is gloriously turned upside down. Your sense of self is reshaped by love and chaos. Without ever asking for it, you found yourself living with a tiny Zen teacher...showing up daily with no filter, no pause, and no regard for adult expectations.

And that's when it began...not the parenting you imagined, but the becoming you never expected. You started growing in ways you didn't know you needed:
More present. More honest.
More human.
More heartbroken.
And more in love than you ever thought possible.

A Similar Thing Happens to Many Teachers

We prepare. We plan. We show up with our whole hearts. Because we love children. That's why we chose this path.

And then comes real life: A child who doesn't respond to our offerings. A lesson that falls flat. A classroom that feels more like a mystery than a map. And we realize that we, too, are being changed.

Working with children stretched me in ways I never expected. I had to let go of needing things to go "right" and learn to lead with presence and patience, not with control.

Flexibility became the teacher. Attunement became the method.
Listening, adjusting, trusting...this is where real learning unfolded way beyond my expectations.

And it's not just parents or teachers...

Aunties, Uncles, Grandparents, Nannies, and all Caregivers...

Children have the power to change anyone who spends meaningful time with them. They invite us to see with new eyes, to play again, and to trust the present. They show us how to live without rushing. How to move from curiosity beyond our old habits.

They move us to our core.

And when we allow that to happen, we change, we learn, we grow alongside them and we join the dance of becoming.

What we all share across homes, cultures, and generations is our love for the young ones in our care. And perhaps one of the greatest gifts we can offer is not found in plans or programs, but in the quiet spaces in between. The unscheduled moments. Those are the times when a young person can breathe, unfold, and simply be. When they can feel themselves. Hear their own thoughts. Explore their curiosities. Touch their place in the world.

Allowing yourself to fully experience a moment with a child is a gift in all directions. It reaches backward to your own younger self, and forward to the adult this child will become. In the here and now, it settles into your nervous system, inviting real-time safety and ease. All of this, simply by letting yourself be here, together, now, in the Zone with your child.

Introduction

This book is a celebration of learning
and a healing between the generations.

In the Zone with Your Child is not a method or a collection of good advice; it's designed to be a companion on your journey with the children in your care and your Inner Child. It's a reminder of how children truly grow and how we can grow alongside them. It invites a different way of being together, one that doesn't rely on control, but on presence, connection, and trust. Because children are not little adults. And most of us are not as grown-up as we like to think.
We are all learning how to be human, together.

There's an old story about six blind mice trying to understand an elephant. One touches the trunk, another the tail, another a leg, and each comes away convinced they understand the whole animal. Yet each has only discovered one part of a much larger reality. The same is true of the themes in this book.

In the Zone with Your Child invites you to move around the whole elephant with eyes wide open, and begin to sense the full shape of these mysteries we call childhood, learning, and growing up. Flow, presence, nervous system safety, learning, companionship, the Inner Child, embodiment, environment, and community are not separate processes. They influence one another, support one another, and continually shape one another.

To understand this larger picture, we will explore each aspect one at a time. Not because life happens in a straight line, but because every journey needs a starting point. And from this wider view, we arrive at the heart of it all. The living force that makes learning possible in the first place: presence.

Presence is the frequency of childhood, and it's also the frequency of adults in our most grounded, joyful, and alive moments. You feel the power of presence most clearly when you find something you *love* to do. This is true for adults, and just as true for children.

When we find something we love, even the simplest things, like making sourdough bread or creating origami sculptures, that's the moment to support it. Because that's the beginning of our deliberate love for learning, our self-motivation, and joy. When we fully dedicate ourselves to an activity, we find ourselves **in the Zone, also known as flow state**, that sweet spot where everything clicks, time disappears, and we surprise ourselves with skills, grit, and finesse beyond what we thought possible.

This phenomenon is being studied across fields, from neuroscience to business leadership, sports psychology to education. But too often, flow state is reduced to a high-productivity mental hack, to a state only experienced in peak moments. But that's only part of the story. Flow didn't emerge from performance science alone. It grew out of research on happiness and meaning, pioneered by Mihály Csíkszentmihályi. Flow is not just a highly focused mind; it is an optimal experience in which every part of us says yes to the same direction. Mind, body, emotions, and soul move as one, like a flock of birds shifting mid-air, effortlessly in sync. In essence, *flow is a state of heightened presence*: without full immersion in the present moment, it could not arise.

And there's one more piece that hasn't received the attention it deserves: children are masters of flow.

Children Are Masters of Flow

As children, we are present by default. We move in and out of the Zone each day, through play, movement, exploration, tinkering, storytelling, building, pretending, and wondering. We become one with an activity, free of self-consciousness, and learn deeply as we're doing it.

This kind of learning, **Flow Learning,** doesn't need to end with childhood. From newborns to teenagers, young adults, grown-ups, and elders: play, hands-on discovery, and flow can remain vital and life-affirming at every stage of life.

This book is for anyone who wants to protect, nurture, and rekindle that inner drive in a child, and in themselves. Whether you're enriching life at home, in schools, community centers, or creating entirely new kinds of schools, Flow

Learning, as described in these pages, opens up a new dimension of joyful growth, filled with empowerment and possibility.

In the Zone With Your Child

When you meet your child in the Zone, playing, creating, marveling, or simply sharing a moment, you're not just making memories; you're healing the child you once were. These moments give you the chance to re-experience what you might have missed or repair old hurts, right inside the living fabric of Now.

For your child, these moments are seeds for the future. Each one helps them build a lifelong inner resource, a sense of flow and self-trust they can return to, no matter what life brings. You show them how to create joy, safety, and possibility from within. This is more than bonding; it's a transformation across generations, rewriting the past and empowering the future, all in one single moment together.

Your Child / Our Child

Throughout this book, "your child" means any child who has walked into your life and your heart...not by blood necessarily, but by bond. Whether you are a parent, grandparent, teacher, caregiver, or simply someone who cherishes the young, every child in your care is a bit *yours* for the time you are together. In those moments, your presence matters and your love leaves an imprint.

As you read, you may remember your own childhood: "your child" also refers to your Inner Child, who is listening, learning, and feeling alongside the child in your care. Your Inner Child needs your love and attention, too, and when both are nurtured, the child in you and the child in your care, generations begin to heal. The cycle of presence and compassion deepens, and a new legacy of trust, creativity, and wholeness is born.

A Living Laboratory of Flow

This work emerged from a living field of study that includes alternative schools, homeschooling communities, unschoolers, summer camps, after-school makerspaces, and flow-friendly classrooms around the world. Over the past decades, countless educators, parents, and life-long learners have contributed to this evolving body of wisdom. We stand at the confluence of positive psychology, polyvagal theory, flow state research, and embodied learning.

But this work also arises from something more subtle and powerful: the clues found in thousands of biographies, memoirs, and interviews with extraordinary people across every field. Whether in sports, the arts, science, or innovation, one theme repeats: someone believed in this person during childhood.

Often, it was a parent who protected the child's spark. Sometimes, it was a grandparent, a coach, a neighbor, or a teacher who saw the child clearly and offered the right kind of support at the right moment. Not always perfectly. Not every day. But enough.

You'll hear it from athletes like Simone Biles, who was raised by grandparents who gave her stability and unconditional love. From musicians like Yo-Yo Ma, who was nurtured in an environment of curiosity, freedom, and respect. From tech innovators like Steve Jobs, who credited a fourth-grade teacher with saving him by simply noticing his brilliance. Or from writers like Maya Angelou, who honored Mrs. Bertha Flowers as the woman who helped her find her voice again.

But protecting the spark of a child isn't always about the child becoming a prodigy, winning medals, or changing the world in obvious ways.
Sometimes, it's simply this:
A grown-up planted the seed that you matter.
That you're allowed to have boundaries.
That you're worthy of love even when you mess up.

Those moments often don't make headlines.
But they change the inner course of a life.

And that's what this book is about...
how you can become that someone for a child...and for yourself.

A Note on Using This Book

This book follows **the arc of what it means to be fully human**, from the brilliance of our minds, to the wisdom of our hearts and the courage of true embodiment.

You may wonder what flow state has to do with being a caretaker, or how your own joy of learning is connected to your child's. The answer is in the journey itself... revealed as you read Part by Part, Invitation by Invitation:

Flow awakens us to what is possible. And it leads us to Presence.

Presence begins with Safety.

Safety opens the door to the Forever Now.

The Forever Now reveals Flow Learning.

Flow Learning helps us become Flow Companions.

Flow Companionship brings us face to face with our Inner Child.

Healing the Inner Child deepens Embodiment.

Embodiment inspires us to create Flow Places.

Flow Places grow into Flow Communities.

And eventually, flow becomes a way of life.

And woven into this journey is something dear to my heart: **Flow Sundays**. An invitation to experiment with community afternoons for children and the Inner Child, to be in the Zone together.

This is the arc of the book. While each Part within it focuses on a different aspect of the journey, all of them are interconnected. **Change in one area creates change in the others. These aspects continually shape, support, and influence one another as part of a single living process...your becoming.**

However, I didn't write this book in a straight line; I sculpted it more like a mosaic, not knowing where each segment lives until it eventually found its place. You are welcome to read it the same way, and let yourself be guided by curiosity. The right passage will find you... and perhaps that's enough for today.

Start experimenting and use this book as a portal to the Zone in your daily life. Explore how it can renew your energy, open your creativity, and strengthen the bond with your child and your inner self.

Rekindle in yourself the same flow state your child, artists, athletes, innovators, and visionaries enjoy when creating their most beautiful work. The state where life itself meets young and old to connect, play, and learn.

May this book be a companion on your journey back to your original Self with ever more wisdom.

So let's begin in the here and now, where presence becomes magic,
and every moment holds the power to transform us all.

With love,
Carmen Gamper
California, 2026

INVITATIONS IN THIS PART:

1 Let Flow Find You Again

2 The Many Expressions of Flow

3 Behind the Scenes

PART ONE

Welcome to the Zone

You've heard the word a thousand times: flow state. Being in the Zone.
But what is flow, really?
Is it a feeling? A brain state? A mystical place
where genius and achievement hold hands?
Or is it something deeper... something at the very pulse of life itself,
available to everyone, not just the high achievers?

In this Part, we'll unravel the mystery and meet the science behind the magic.
We'll look at how brain waves and neurochemicals do a happy dance,
how this state boosts learning, confidence, and even mental health.

You'll discover why top athletes, artists, musicians, scientists,
and high achievers in every field train to live here...
and why your child is already wired for it.

We'll explore what happens when you and your child enter that timeless state
of deep presence. You'll see how flow teaches, reveals, heals, and transforms.
And why your child is already an expert in it.
Let's begin the journey! Let's dive in...

1

INVITATION 1
Let Flow Find You Again

There's a feeling you've had before. Maybe it was while painting as a child, dancing, or working late on a project that mattered to you.

Time disappeared. Thoughts quieted. You were fully in it...*in the Zone.*

Psychologists call it flow; a state of deep focus, natural motivation, and inner ease. In flow, body and mind work together. You feel alert, alive, and fully yourself.

Children live much closer to this state than we do. They enter flow naturally, when they play. There's no pressure. Just presence. Just doing what they love.

And then slowly, it slips. Pressure enters. Schedules. Praise and performance. Flow gives way to stress, not just for us, but for children too.

Remember what it feels like, or do you feel it often?
When your whole being is immersed in something you love. When your hands know what to do without overthinking. When hours pass like minutes. When it's not only about doing something efficiently, but about enjoying it.

And perhaps you know how wonderful it is to share that very thing you love with another person, perhaps a child. Not only to teach it, but to share your delight.

Even simple acts of creativity done whole-heartedly, in flow, anchor us, whether with children or on our own. They remind us what it feels like to be *whole* in our own company.

This is Flow

You'll know you're in the Zone when something inside you says, YES.
You're focused... deeply so.
There's no watcher, no doer.
Just being. Just this.

An inner stillness where doing, playing, creating,
learning, connecting, and contemplating unfold as if by magic.
You're not planning the next step.
Something deeper is moving you.
Mind and body align, moving together, supporting each other.

Time slows down... or disappears.
You might feel like you're riding a current, where everything just makes sense.
Even the hard parts feel right. Challenges become invitations, not threats, and
the effort itself feels strangely satisfying.

You stop watching yourself.
You *are* yourself.
And this isn't magic from the outside,
it's more of you.
Fully present, undistracted, alive...the state you knew so well as a child.

Whether old or young, proficient or beginner,
what unites us in the Zone is the courage to let go
and trust the body and our whole being.
The intelligence we access in the Zone sees more, moves faster and responds
with an ease conscious effort can't replicate.

This often leads to peak performance
but that's just a wonderful side effect.
Flow is about the journey.

Flow Is About the Journey

We forget this so easily. The world trains us to look ahead toward outcomes, goals, results, proof. But flow doesn't live in the future. It lives in the only place that ever truly exists: this moment.

Each moment is a small universe, a chance to drop into your breath, your curiosity, your hands, your senses. When you are in the Zone, you're not trying to get anywhere. You're already there.

And something beautiful happens when you allow that...
The outcome stops holding power over you.
It stops defining your worth.
It stops deciding whether you "succeeded" or "failed."

Because when you spend your time doing something you genuinely love,
you've already won.
You've given yourself the richest thing a human can receive:
the experience of being fully yourself, happy in your own company.

This is why children don't measure their play by the finished product.

And this is why adults can return to joy the moment they stop chasing and start inhabiting.

Flow isn't about where you're going.
Flow is about how it feels to be on the way.

And when the way feels meaningful,
nourishing, and alive,
the destination can only add to the abundance
you already carry inside.

The Spark of Joyful Learning

Before learning becomes a subject, a duty, or a measure of success, it begins as joy.

From the very beginning, children experience the struggles of learning and the breakthroughs of mastery, such as holding a spoon or throwing a ball.

But they don't set out to master things; they set out to experience the joy of flow, and flow creates the ideal conditions for learning:
attention, repetition, feedback, and delight.

Every true master of their craft, whether in sports, science, or art,
has something in common with your child.
They've spent time in the Zone.
They've felt the joy of doing something for its own sake.
They've practiced, not (only) because they had to, but because they wanted to.

The deeper source of that joy is agency: the sense that you chose this. Agency doesn't mean you must invent every step yourself. You can be in full agency while someone else, for instance a coach, a teacher, a trainer, gives you instructions. Flow doesn't require independence; it requires consent.

It means that your inner world is aligned. Your body, your instincts, your inner child, your cautious parts, even your inner critic are all in agreement. They're saying, "Yes, this is the thing we want to do." And that choice is what opens the door to joy, and to your creative spark.

The spark is not reserved for prodigies.
It's built into all of us, and it's especially lit when we're young.

This is our sense of worthiness.

The sense of capability that rises when you trust yourself enough to try something new, and then keep going. You go deeper.
You get good enough and flow takes over.

Practice becomes so fulfilling it becomes devotion.

True masters are always learning and playing, and that is their joy.

No matter if you or your child become masterful at something,
the most important thing is spending time in the Zone,
side by side or on your own, because this is where we can receive the gifts each moment offers.

Building a Home Inside

So many masters of flow never aimed for success. They followed their spark. And fame, recognition, legacy was a byproduct of their deep engagement and love of the craft.

We see this in great musicians like Paul McCartney, who once said:

"We were just kids playing music. We weren't trying to be legends.
We just followed what felt good."

It's the same for most artists; Georgia O'Keeffe once explained that she could say things with color and shapes that she had no words for.

And so many athletes feel the same way, for instance, Michael Jordan said in his Hall of Fame speech that the game was his sanctuary, a place to go when he had nothing else.

Even for the most famous masters of flow, the Zone isn't about an outcome; it is still about following a truth within themselves.

Whether you become an expert in one field or keep sampling flow activities all your life, you are building an inner resource and deepening your sense of self.

For young children, this happens every day. When they play, create, tinker, and explore, they are building a stable identity from the inside out.

The same current that moves your child to build a pillow fort is the one that carried Mozart, Serena Williams, Yo-Yo Ma, and every master you've ever admired.

Flow is not a trick of the mind.

It's the frequency of creation.

It flows through nature.

It flows through music.

It flows through children.

And it flows through each of us,

when we feel safe and present enough to let it.

From here, flow will take many forms.
In your life. In your child's life.
In the quiet, the messy, the miraculous, and the mundane.
Let's begin to notice them all.
And this is the next Invitation: The Many Expressions of Flow in Our Lives.

2

INVITATION 2

The Many Expressions of Flow in Our Lives

Flow is a universal experience that arises in infinite forms, depending on the person, the moment, and the energy behind it. Sometimes it's a deep stillness, and other times a wild current. But no matter its form, flow is always a homecoming...a return to your own rhythm and breath.

There's something magnetic about a person in flow, at any age. When someone is fully present and at ease with themselves, others feel it. Their grounded aliveness lifts the space around them. Flow doesn't persuade or perform. It simply is. And in being fully itself, it draws others into presence as well.

Here are four common ways flow shows up in our lives:

    1) Stillness Flow

    2) Creative Expression Flow

    3) Movement Flow

    4) Mind Flow

As you read the following descriptions, think of which ones feel most alive in you and your child right now. Which ones would you love to welcome more of?

1) Stillness Flow

This flow is available in the simplest corners of everyday life... in the Zone with your child, or delighted in your own activity.

It's the place in you where the current of life moves without hurry. Here, the noise of the world cannot enter, and you return to the rhythm of your own heartbeat.

Activities may start as a chore and become unexpectedly satisfying, even meditative. While folding laundry, you might find a rhythm, the repetitive motions calming your mind.

In this state, the nervous system shifts into the parasympathetic state, rest and digest. There is no search for meaning because you are the meaning, right here, in this moment of being alive.

A master of this kind of flow was Thich Nhat Hanh, the great Zen teacher whose voice reminded us that peace is every step. And you might see this flow in a child sitting peacefully watching a snail. This is flow as restorative presence and meditation, where we feel completely safe, and allowed to just *be*.

2) Creative Expression Flow

This is the flow of playful creation, invention, and expression. Whether you're crafting, writing, building, cooking, playing an instrument, or dancing, it's rarely a straight line. Flow likes to zig and zag, carrying you through moments of effort, pause, and discovery.

Like when a child makes a paper airplane or you're learning a new instrument: trying new moves, testing, practicing, adjusting, and sticking with the process. The joy comes from learning as you go, being flexible and open to surprise. In this kind of flow, your brain stays engaged, plastic and adaptive, responding in real time to what's needed.

Sometimes you're fully in the Zone, gliding scissors along a perfect curve. Other times you're puzzling over a tricky step. You start enjoying the process, and let yourself move between trial and triumph, frustration and fascination.

This is flow as creative exploration. It lives in curiosity, flexibility, and the willingness to be shaped by what you're making, even as you shape it.

3) Movement Flow

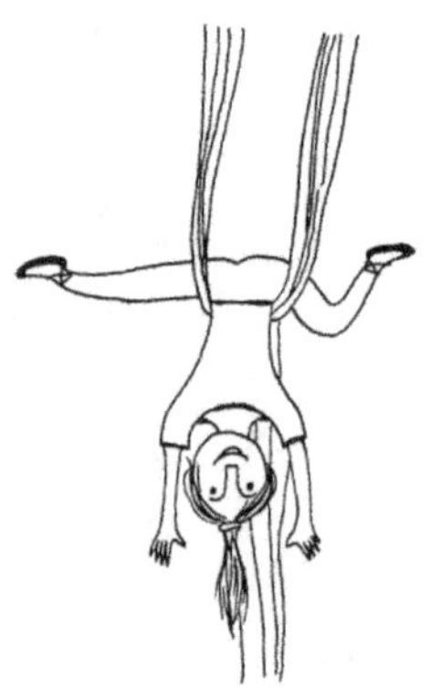

Movement is one of the most direct doorways into the Zone. Stand on one foot for a moment, try to balance, and you're already much more present. Playful movement can drop you into flow just as easily as structured movement. Wiggling, stretching, and swaying just because it feels good is every bit as powerful as a choreography, a gymnastics routine, or a martial arts form. Whether spontaneous or scripted, movement gathers the mind and body into one clear channel.

Some kinds of movement come with speed, risk, and precision. In these moments, your nervous system is highly activated, but not dysregulated, it's locked in and alert. It's the surge that parkour athletes , skiers, or breakdancers know well, the state where there's no room for doubt, only quick reflexes and pure instinct.

Children seek this often in climbing, racing, and testing their limits. When accessed skillfully, this state leads to extraordinary levels of focus, courage, and embodied intelligence.

There's an even sharper form of flow in this category: Survival flow.
Sometimes the moment hurls you into it because your life depends on it. There's no warm-up, no gradual merging. Mind, emotions, body all locked into alignment by urgency. It might be a driver taking corners at impossible speed, a rescuer pulling someone from the water. It's an assault of presence: clarity so sharp it cuts through fear, vision so wide it takes in every angle. A second stretches long enough for a dozen decisions, a minute contracts into a single, unbroken action. You are the flow, catapulted into it by the gravity of now-or-never.

4) Mind Flow

Sometimes, flow lives in the spark behind your eyes. You're writing a story, solving a math problem, imagining a world no one's ever seen, and something clicks. Time dissolves. The voice of doubt goes silent. You're not thinking about thinking. You're inside the thought itself, riding it like a wave.

It is imagination and it's also more. It's a mind set free. It's the mathematician who suddenly sees the harmony inside a pattern. The composer who hears a melody no one has played yet. The writer who receives the first line of a book as if it were handed to them. The painter who closes their eyes and sees the finished canvas before a single brushstroke falls. It is the moment of the "download" and the "lightbulb," when something larger than your ordinary thinking moves through you and leaves something real behind.

Children are natural inhabitants of this space. You see a cardboard box and they see a spaceship. Their minds roam freely in ways that build resilience, creativity, and the capacity to solve problems.

Adults can return here too. It asks only that you make a little room for your inner self, for play, for brainstorming, for sitting with a question and trusting what arrives. Einstein called imagination more important than knowledge, and his thought experiments, including riding alongside a beam of light, rewrote our understanding of the universe. He was, in *mind flow*, playing.

Mind flow is the free sky: boundless, creative, and always waiting for you to look up.

Flow Will Surprise You!

Flow works with everything you've learned, your muscle memory, your skills, your knowledge, and uses it to create something new...often something sensational! It grabs the mind by the hand and says, "Come on, let's go!"

If you're a skier, flow will take your well-trained legs and say, "Let's do the most epic run of your life."
If you're a writer, it'll grab your words, toss them in the air like juggling balls, and see what lands on the page.

Beatrix Potter said about her writing process:
"There is something so delicious about writing the first words of a story. You never quite know where they'll take you."

Flow knows the rules. It also knows when to break them.
So often, flow doesn't care where you thought you were going.
It's rarely here to get you there faster...it's taking you somewhere better.

Robin Williams improvised so wildly as the Genie in the animation *Aladdin* that entire scenes were built around his spontaneous genius.

During a live performance, Jacob Collier, the beloved British musician known for his extraordinary improvisations, heard a cell phone ring. He smiled, wove the ringtone into his melody, and kept going. He turned an interruption into art.

That's what flow is.
Not avoiding disruption. Not "good vibes only."
But *this*: Presence so deep it can metabolize anything.
When your day rings off-key, when the plan is ruined... flow includes the noise.
And plays anyway.

And Then There Are Moments of Flow...

Sun-warmed, velvet peach
a laugh, juice running sideways.
Your child's smile finds yours.

A flash of presence so alive, so real, it cracks open time.

A baby's first laugh.
A snowflake landing on your nose.
The hush before a concert begins.

These are moments of flow...brief, electric, sacred.
Life itself, so sweet, so beautiful, so big, so intense,
it beckons us out of our heads and into the now.

Suddenly, your breath catches, your eyes widen... wow... *You're alive.*

And the incredible part is...
young children live like this all the time.
They're awake enough to catch it
when life decides to shimmer.

We can too. Even if just for seconds,
in the space between thoughts.
These moments are gifts...
love notes falling like petals
through the cracks in our ordinary days.

Flow is Our Birthright

Flow is a natural birthright woven into every child's and every grown-ups being, waiting patiently to be remembered. Even if the world distracts or pressures us away from it, the pathway home is always there.

And now, as we turn the page, we shift from the many expressions of flow to what makes them possible. We've looked at the outer shape. Next, we explore the inner workings. We step behind the scenes.

3

INVITATION 3
Behind the Scenes

Flow looks effortless on the outside, but there's much more happening than meets the eye. Flow is a coordinated shift inside the whole system, as mind, body, attention, emotion, all align in one meaningful moment.

This Invitation takes you on a backstage tour of the core ingredients that make flow possible. Whether it's a child lost in play or a jazz legend on stage, the internal patterns are surprisingly similar. Let's peek behind the scenes.

Mechanics and Magic

How we get into the Zone is as diverse as humanity itself. Perfecting muscle memory does not guarantee flow, but it builds the skills flow may later use to play with.

As a child, I spent years training in figure skating and taking flute lessons. I put in the hours and gained decent skills. The muscle memory was there, the control was there, but I was tense, self-conscious, and trying to "get it right." Looking back, I realize I never quite entered the Zone. Why? Because I didn't enjoy it, and it wasn't my choice to be there. As an adult, I discovered the Native American flute and now I use my childhood muscle memory to play it intuitively and joyfully.

If someone has great skills but no joy, they may be efficient, but without the spark of flow. If someone is a happy amateur, they may not have perfect skills, but possibly enough for flow to take over.

Some children and adults enter flow without any training at all. They pick up a harmonica, a pencil, or a ball of clay, and create something beautiful. They are guided by their own flow, their intuitive system that expresses patterns, rhythm, and emotion all at once. This happens more often than we assume: a child suddenly reads without a formal lesson, someone picks up a guitar and can somehow play. At any age we may discover a talent that seems to have been there all along. This is when flow precedes skill. A striking example is a child prodigy like Mozart, composing music before he could fully read or write.

When a natural doer begins formal lessons, they may slow down at first, stumble, and feel clumsy, because they start thinking about each movement instead of letting it flow. It's like learning the grammar of a language you already speak. With practice, the analytical and intuitive systems begin to cooperate, and flow returns.

Flow reveals itself differently in everyone. Some discover joy first and practice follows. Others build skills first, and joy arrives as mastery deepens. What matters is the blend: practice builds skills, joy gives energy, and a sense of agency.

You can have two people performing the exact same movement, the same jump on the ice, or the same melody on the flute, and both can be technically perfect. But while one feels flat, the other feels like a revelation. We saw this in figure skater Alysa Liu, whose joy on the ice radiated around the world. Her excellence didn't hide her joy; it amplified it, proving that discipline can be joyful.

Whether you're a curious beginner or a seasoned artist, if you love what you're doing, flow can find you.

The greatest advice I ever received was this:
"Stop trying to "get it right" and start being really present
with the part that is already joyful for you."

Tending the Body While in Flow
*Flow's Little Asterisk

For people of all ages, flow is deeply nourishing. It's where we feel most at home in ourselves, doing what we love. But there's one small asterisk to this glorious state.

P.S. While basking in the Zone, please remember: Your human body loves flow but needs basic maintenance. Thank you for your cooperation.

Experienced flow learners naturally meet their genuine needs. They pause, drink, snack, rest, and return with ease. But that takes time. Children, and those just beginning to reclaim flow, often forget their body's needs.

Take Luca, the passionate potter. He's at his wheel for hours, shaping clay. Only when he finally stands up does he notice: his legs are numb, and...wait! Did the sun set already?

Or Sophie, the seven-year-old architect. She's been building a magnificent pillow kingdom all afternoon. Only when someone calls her name does she realize she's so hungry, her stomach is growling.

The more aware we become, the easier it is to listen within, to notice the thirst before the headache and pause for food before the crash. To rest before we fall apart. This is why children benefit from a grown-up who will occasionally check in: "Want to take a break?"
"Would a snack help right now?"
Or, if you're solo, set a timer to remind yourself,
"Am I thirsty? Hungry? Do I need a stretch?"

Over time, this awareness becomes second nature. You'll stretch, sip, breathe, and return, still in the Zone, but fully resourced. Because flow isn't meant to separate us from the body. It's meant to bring us home to it.

Simple Presence Vs. Flow State

Both, being fully present and flow state interrupt the mind's habitual thinking patterns, called the default mode network (DMN). However, in simple presence the mind is still efforting and analyzing, while in flow the intuitive systems lead.

When we become really present with what is *right here right now*, the prefrontal cortex, the part of our brain that plans and evaluates is still active. It can guide decisions, make sense of sensations, and give meaning to experiences.

Flow is different. When presence and skill meet in that sweet spot described by Mihály Csíkszentmihályi, the prefrontal cortex goes quiet in what neuroscientists call *transient hypofrontality*. The lead is handed over to older, faster brain circuits, such as the motor cortex, cerebellum, and implicit memory, the body's deep store of learned skills and movement patterns that operate below conscious thought. So the violin riff, the downhill turn, or the perfect sentence seems to *move through* rather than being directed by conscious command. The body's larger intelligence takes the wheel while the analytical mind fades into the background.

Presence is a clear lake: you can see the bottom and choose where to swim.

Flow is a river: you are the water, moving without commentary.

And beyond these two states, there is awareness.
Your awareness is the vast ocean within which both the lake and the river exist.

The Brain in Flow

Brain scans and other neuroimaging techniques show that during flow the prefrontal cortex is less active, brainwaves follow specific patterns, and a cocktail of feel-good chemicals floods the brain. Let's look at what happens inside the body and brain when we enter the Zone: how thinking quiets, senses heighten, and joy, focus, and curiosity rise.

The Prefrontal Cortex: Flow's Quiet Guide

Normally, the prefrontal cortex (PFC) runs the show: planning, making decisions, and controlling impulses. But during flow, it is quiet. This temporary shift, called transient hypofrontality, lets other brain regions step forward. Intuition and immersion take the lead. We respond with our whole selves: senses, emotions, instinct, and intuition.

After flow, the PFC returns, ready to help us reflect and learn. Flow isn't the absence of thought; it's thought aligned with presence. In these moments, the PFC becomes more of a wise guide who trusts the moment.

Brainwaves During Flow

Flow brings the brain into the alpha-theta range of brain waves, which are linked to calm focus and dreamy immersion. Alpha waves hum, "You're safe. Keep going." Theta whispers, "Try this. Trust this."

Some flow activities may include alert beta waves; these states are more alert, but still harmonious. The key difference is that, unlike stress or fear-driven beta waves, flow keeps the system integrated. There's focus, not panic.

The Symphony of Flow Chemicals

Flow is a chemical symphony. Each neurochemical adds to the music:

◊ Dopamine, the violin. "This is exciting, keep going!" Fuels curiosity and reward.

◊ Norepinephrine, the trumpet. "Stay with it." Sharpens focus and urgency.

◊ Adrenaline, the snare drum. "Now! Move!" Boosts energy in high-stakes moments.

◊ Anandamide, the flute. "Let go. You're safe." Eases stress and invites play.

◊ Glutamate, the piano. "Let's make sense of this." Builds new connections fast.

◊ Serotonin, the cello. "You're okay. Breathe." Grounds emotions.

◊ Oxytocin, the harp. "You belong here." Fosters connection and trust.

All of this unfolds beneath the surface, yet what we feel is simple. We feel more ourselves. Thought quiets, the senses awaken, and the whole system begins to move in harmony. The brain, body, and emotions no longer compete, they cooperate.

This is flow: not something we create through effort, but something that emerges when we feel safe, engaged, and fully here. The science describes it, but the experience is unmistakable: a quiet sense that everything is working together, and that, in this moment, we belong exactly where we are.

Digital Flow ~ The Pixel Portal

Why Screen Flow Feels Good, But isn't the Same

When approached with awareness, screens can offer immersive experiences that build attention and spark learning. But unlike embodied forms of flow, this one requires care. Too much, too fast, and it tips into overstimulation or dissociation.

Digital activities can trigger flow-like brain patterns, such as dopamine surges and reduced prefrontal activity, but they differ from the embodied, full-sensory flow of real-world play and creation.

In screen flow, much of the sensory-motor feedback of a full-body experience is bypassed. The body often stays still while the mind races. This can feel great in the moment, but may lead to depletion later. After screen flow, we often feel dazed, overstimulated, or numbed, even if the experience was fun.

So while screen-based activities can feel like flow, they are best balanced with embodied experiences. When we move, breathe, or feel our feet on the ground, the nervous system finds its anchor again. Also creative integration after screen time, like drawing or talking about what was seen, can bring children and grown-ups back to themselves.

Once children are used to screen flow, switching back to hands-on activities can feel frustrating at first. Of course...because there's less dopamine, less instant rewards, and no fast-forward button.

It may take something truly exciting to entice a child back into the joy of embodiment, like a camping trip with fire-making, an adventure playground, a puppy, or any activity that stirs real-life curiosity. But often after a period of boredom and integration the magic of embodied flow returns.

Then There Is Awareness...

Beyond brain waves and neurochemicals, even beyond presence and flow, there is *your full being* at the heart of every moment: your awareness. It is the loving observer behind experience, the part that feels the thrill of skiing down a slope, or the warmth of hugging a friend.

Awareness is harder to locate in brain scans because it isn't tied to a single region. It's more like a field, something that emerges across the whole system. It becomes easier to sense when the mind grows quiet and the body feels safe.

Joseph Chilton Pearce, author of *Magical Child* described how, in states of safety, the prefrontal cortex relaxes into what he called the "angel lobes," a softened, receptive version of our analytical brain that allows loving awareness to come forward.

This kind of awareness doesn't disappear in hard moments. Even in chaos, even when you're overwhelmed, there is often a flicker of it, a kind presence that watches, feels, and stays.It observes, but not critically. Everything that evaluates, corrects, or monitors belongs to the analytical mind.

Awareness doesn't zoom in to analyze.

It is expansive. It holds space. It is benevolent.

It is a caring witness within.

Over time, this part can grow stronger, becoming your Inner Parent, your steady companion, and your closest ally.

Developing a gentle, supportive awareness of our body and our surroundings is one of the most important things we can do.

It helps us know when we are in the Zone.

It helps us feel the needs of our bodies, our emotions, and the children in our care.

It helps us stay human in the moment.

It is awareness that allows us to say:

"I am here and this is good."

When Flow Is a Refuge

Not all flow arises from joy. Sometimes it appears as a way to cope with something too overwhelming to face.

A child might build Lego towers for hours, not only out of passion, but because it's the one place they feel safe or in control. A grown-up might lose themselves in drawing, music, or running, not just to improve, but to find emotional shelter. Even screens and scrolling, often judged harshly, can offer temporary regulation when emotions feel too big or too raw to face alone.

This kind of flow isn't "wrong." It might be exactly what's needed in that moment. When we don't yet have the tools or support to face what's rising, the nervous system seeks rhythm and focus to survive. This, too, is intelligence... not the thriving kind, but the surviving kind. And sometimes, survival is enough.

Later, when safety returns, we can come closer to the deeper flow that heals. Until then, we offer compassion to the child seeking refuge,...or to ourselves:
"This feels safer right now. And that's okay. When you're ready, we can look underneath together."

Flow and Mental Health

Mental health is not just the absence of anxiety or depression. It is the presence of curiosity, connection, resilience, and the ability to be with yourself, or return to yourself after hard moments. Flow supports all of these.

When we're immersed in meaningful activity, we get a break from overthinking. The inner critic quiets. The nervous system settles. Even brief moments of deep engagement can shift us from overwhelm toward steadiness.

This is not a small thing. For many people, flow is one of the few places where the weight lifts for a moment, and they relax.

For some, especially those living with trauma, anxiety, or depression, the path back to this steadiness may take time and support. Flow is a reminder that the mind still holds this capacity. The seeds are there.

Children need this refuge daily. So do adults. A child rolling on the floor, building a fort, or staring at the ceiling may be regulating more than we realize. An adult running, dancing, baking, or sitting with a cup of tea may be doing the same.

Regular return to flow builds mental health from the inside out. Not by fixing what is broken, but by reminding the whole system what it feels like to be at ease.

Calibrating Ourselves for Flow

The more often we enter flow, the more the nervous system begins to recognize it as a "safe zone." This is especially powerful in childhood, when the brain is most open to shaping itself around experience.

When a child spends hours in deep play, the brain's reward system lights up, weaving those moments together with an internal "yes." Studies show that early playful exploration lays a stronger foundation for adult expertise than rigid training alone. Childhood joy can become the soil for future skills.

And it is never too late.

At any age, each time we play, move, create, or explore without pressure,
we strengthen these neural pathways.
Every playful moment becomes a message to the nervous system:
this is a safe, nurturing, and meaningful place to be.

And beyond the specific skills linked to an activity,
something deeper is forming.
Flow builds a portable inner toolkit. We are learning how to steady our breath, focus attention, take in new information, and move with intention.

These metaskills travel with us, making it easier to get into flow,
no matter what we do.

Over time, the body begins to recognize subtle cues such as a deep breath,
an inner smile, or a familiar movement, as a green light to begin.
This is how we calibrate for flow:
by returning to it, again and again.

Closing Reflection Part One

Flow is not one thing.
It's many languages of presence.
Sometimes quiet. Sometimes wild.
But always bringing us back to life.

Each person's relationship with flow is unique,
shaped by their rhythm, their wiring, their wonder.
But beneath every version of it, something steady pulses:

Whether it rises as creativity, stillness, mastery, or refuge, every form of flow is a
doorway that reconnects us with the *NOW*.

When you create space for unhurried time, that's the place where flow begins.
This is what we'll explore next: Presence in the Forever Now.

PART TWO

It All Starts With Presence

There's a place your child already knows, where imagination flows like breath and time stretches like sunlight across a warm floor.

It's this moment, the one right here, where attention and joy meet.

You used to live there, too.

In these pages, we'll return to this place together.

You'll discover that presence isn't a fleeting second, it's a frequency.

A state of grace that's always available.

It's the portal to the Zone, where flow, creativity, and connection all begin in the safety of now.

Your child is waiting for you there.

These pages will help you find your way back, too.

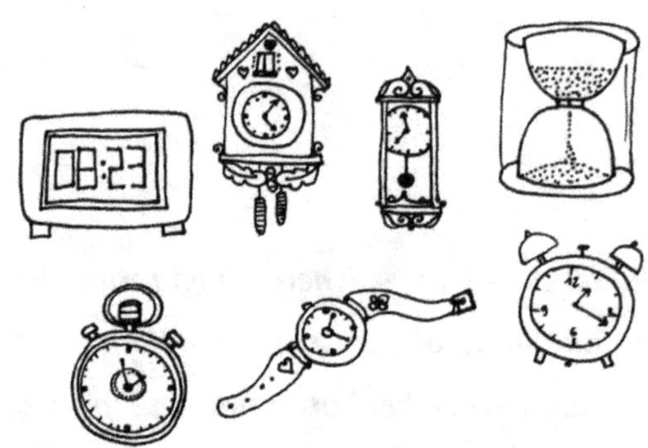

It's always now.

4

INVITATION 4

Rediscovering the Forever Now

The Place Where Children Live

There's the now we all know. The now of spilled cereal and dentist waiting rooms.
The now of checking the time, of half-listening, of moving through the motions.
This is the ongoing stream of moments that mostly asks for our survival.
It's real, and it matters. But it is not where transformation lives.

And then... there's the *Forever Now, the place where children live.*
The Forever Now is the threshold to the Zone.
It's the golden ring of presence where time softens its grip
and everything feels more alive.

The Forever Now is a shift in frequency and a remembering.
It's your spirit settling into your bones.
It's the only place where you can ever truly meet your child
and, for that matter, anyone.

It's when a child looks up and sees that you are truly here.
It's where flow can take over. Where connection can root.
Where learning and healing are possible.

The Forever Now in Our Daily Lives

There is a paradox we live with as humans.

This world, it hums with longing.

Always in motion, never done.

Always becoming, unfolding, reaching, spiraling onward.

Constantly solving, fixing, striving...

It can feel like we are never quite there.

But then, sometimes without effort, without warning
you get a glimpse of the Forever Now...

You find yourself watching leaves dance in the wind.

Or stirring soup with a sense of reverence you didn't plan.

Or holding your child's gaze and realizing that nothing else exists.

Nothing is missing. There's no spiral, no race.

It's the space you enter when you're painting, baking,

or holding someone who's crying, or crying yourself,

and you forget everything else but what's real in that moment.

Just a quiet marveling: "Hmm... that felt right."

In these moments, you remember that you're okay, right now, right here.

Now, you're no longer managing time, you're meeting life.

You're in a frequency where you slow down enough to say:

"Yes. I'm really here now.
With me. With this. With you."

It may seem at first like stepping into the Forever Now
is a way of avoiding life, turning your back on planning and responsibility.
Many have been taught that stillness is laziness, that presence is avoidance,
and joy is irresponsible.

But in time, you may begin to sense the deeper truth:
The Forever Now is not an escape.
It's the ground beneath everything.
It's the realest thing there is.

It is not turning away from life; it is turning toward it so fully that you dissolve
the illusion of control... and suddenly something inside you knows
what to do next.

The Forever Now Stretches Deep and Wide

The Forever Now is a place beyond linear time.
It's when you anchor so fully in the now that time stops being a concern.
This isn't a loss of time, but a return to real time.
A return to each moment, no matter how long.
To the kind of time we experienced as children,
when an afternoon could last forever
and five minutes in a classroom felt like an eternity.

Presence Tunes Us
Into the Great Human Symphony

The Forever Now doesn't only stretch wide, it stretches deep.
When you enter it, you're not just present with your child.
You're present with everyone who's ever sat by a fire.
With every child who's ever picked up a stone.
With every parent who's ever rocked a baby in the stillness of night.

The Forever Now is where we meet the souls of those who've lived before
or live far away through their art, their poetry, and their wisdom.

You're not simply listening or reading, you're tuning in.

A beautiful example is music... As cellist Steven Isserlis shares in a BBC segment, "You're More Musical Than You Think," "When you play Beethoven, you can get to know him, his incredible spirit that could not be broken by anything."

Through music, you enter a dimension where time folds,
and the composer becomes present.

When you and your child sit together in presence,
you become part of this great tapestry.
You feel connected across centuries and countries.
You understand that wonder, love, and creativity are timeless.
They are universal languages. And that nothing real is ever lost.

In the Now, We Are All Ageless

Flow has no age. In this open, living quantum field
you can touch the past and the future at once.
A three-year-old can play the piano with the soul of a seasoned musician.
An adult can lose all sense of time while drawing, just like a child.
A senior can feel ageless again, transported by music or the scent of a childhood
fragrance. And a child can speak with the wisdom of an old sage.
In the Zone, age dissolves. Presence is all that remains.

The Forever Now Isn't Just a Fleeting Moment

It's all there is.
It's the womb of existence.
The eternal, humming backdrop to everything that's ever happened,
is happening, or will happen.

But it's also wildly simple. So simple your mind will try to complicate it,

decorate it, label it, or sell it. But truly? The Forever Now can't be bought.
It can only be entered.

Every experience you've ever had occurred in the Forever Now.
Even your memories and your imagination? Accessed now.
Even your dreams? Dreamed now.
You can think about past or future, but the experience of thinking only happens
here and now.

You Are the Key

The Forever Now is the doorway to your creativity.
To your freedom. To everything that's ever nourished you.
And this door is always open.
You don't need a key. You are the key.

Some doors open with a giggle.
Some with a deep breath.
Some with a quiet surrender.
Some with a silly muffin dance or a perfect piano melody.
But they all lead to the same place: this moment,
alive and glowing, where you and your child can meet soul to soul.

The Forever Now Doesn't Need Fixing

And here's a paradox, because all the greatest truths are paradoxical:
You create the Now and you receive it at the same time.

Your mind often tries to improve the now:
"This moment would be better if I had a croissant... or a different childhood."
But the now is already whole. It doesn't ask for editing.
It just asks: "Are you here with me?"

And yes… there's always that little flaw.
That soft crack. That unanswered prayer.
And that is where the light comes in.

In Japanese philosophy, this is called *wabi-sabi*, the beauty of imperfection.
It says: "This chipped bowl, this asymmetrical flower,
this moment that slipped through your fingers, this is where the sacred lives."

It Is Your Home, Patiently Waiting

The Forever Now belongs to all of us. It doesn't matter who you are,
where you come from, or what your story has been.
It's not something only the enlightened, the healed, the calm, or the "spiritual"
get to enter. And it's not only for children.

Everyone enters it in different moments in their lives, sometimes because they're
hurting, sometimes because they're curious, sometimes because life cracks them
open in ways they never expected.
This home is always here, patiently waiting with open arms for all of us.

It's the natural human state beneath all the noise.
It is the ground beneath your feet, the breath that never leaves you.

And the moment you step into it, you remember:
you were never truly separate, never truly lost, you just forgot for a moment.
The Forever Now has been here all along,
holding you, holding your child, holding us all.

Get a taste of it right now by hugging yourself and saying,
"Welcome home, Love. I missed you. I'm here now."

Disclaimer: Being Fully Present Doesn't Mean Zoning Out

Let's pause for a quick note on what the Forever now is not...

Sometimes people mistake "being present," or "going with the flow" for doing whatever feels good and forgetting about responsibilities. But flow without integrity isn't flow, it's just impulsivity in disguise.

Deep presence is expanded awareness:
of yourself, others, the moment, and the whole environment.

It's like being a sailor at sea, who knows at all times where true north is,
how strong the wind is, from which direction it blows, the condition of the sails,
and the shape of the waves ahead. They are deeply immersed and fully aware.
They don't forget their surroundings; they become one with them.

That's presence: when you're tracking the whole field:

- your energy and the energy of the child and others around you

- the time of day and the commitments you made

- the movements in the environment

- what's needed to enter flow or transition out of it

- what's needed for your body and the child's body

Presence is the capacity to feel more, hear more, and see more.
It means asking: "What is the most loving, adequate response available here?"
Presence with children invites us into a flow that's honest, grounded,
and full of love.

So How Do We Enter the Forever Now?

The Forever Now sounds beautiful, and it is. But in the swirl of everyday life,
it's not always easy to access.

With so many things pulling on our attention,
presence can feel elusive, sometimes even impossible. You might ask,
"How can I be present when the world feels frightening,
and my mind keeps pulling me into vigilance?"

Presence isn't denial; it's discernment.
Fear, even worry, can bring important information.
But it's not meant to become the atmosphere of your inner and outer home.

You can listen for its message, acknowledge it, by writing it down
or, ideally, doing something about it, and then learn to return to safety.

That return is a nervous-system skill, and it protects your ability to learn, play,
heal, and trust life. You can care deeply without living in alarm.

When we give the nervous system what it needs, the gates of the Forever Now
swing wide open. And that return begins in the body. In the nervous system,
which is where we go next.

Understanding the ways of the nervous system allows us to reap the deep,
sustaining benefits of presence.

5

INVITATION 5

Presence Begins in the Nervous System

Most of us have developed a habit of worry. We feed a constant loop of anxiety, huddled in the shadows of "what if" and "did you hear."

Anxiety is a habit of the nervous system, but so is presence. And that is good news, because habits can change. At first, the peace of the Forever Now might feel foreign, even startling. But slowly, step by step, you get used to it.

When you spend more time in the Forever Now, you don't just start to think differently; you enter a new *physiological* reality. You are teaching your body that it is safe to be here and that changes your breathing, digestion, musculature, and posture. You realize that presence is not a spiritual concept first, it is a biological one. And from there, the joy of being alive comes back within reach.

The Trust Fall Into Presence

No matter our age, staying in the Forever Now and experiencing flow is a kind of trust fall...we must follow curiosity into a place where we are not fully in control. All healing and learning arise only when we feel *safe enough*. Safe enough to relax, to be curious, and to allow novelty. When challenge feels possible because of inner and outer resources.

Even the smallest signs of danger, real or imagined, conscious or unconscious, activate the body's habitual survival reactions. Sometimes our nervous system gears up to fight, hide, or flee, or sometimes it shuts us down. Either way, the body is trying to keep us safe.

So many of the nervous system habits we carry were formed in our earliest years. How often did we feel safe enough to follow curiosity into the unknown?
How often did we get to trust fall into flow, without feeling interrupted, shamed, or abandoned?

Our children ask us with their whole being, every day, "Am I safe here? Is it okay to be myself?" They constantly scan for cues, such as a smile or a kind voice. Sometimes they reach for us with joy, sometimes with protest, and always they're asking:
"Is your heart open to me? Are we in tune? Can I see myself reflected in you?"

When the answer is yes, their energy opens. When the answer feels uncertain, they tighten, withdraw, protest, or over-adapt. This isn't misbehavior. It's communication.

And as adults, our own nervous systems may sometimes feel taxed or uncertain, too. This is simply the dance of two beings seeking safety together.

That's why emotional safety isn't extra.
It is the bedrock of presence.

You might look around and say, "But my home is peaceful. My classroom is organized. My workplace is kind. We are safe here." And you are right. Logically, you are. But this is a primal sense of safety that lives below rational thinking.

It is a subterranean current flowing beneath our conscious thoughts, a "neuroception" that we must learn to tune into. Because the nervous system doesn't read a room with logic; it seeks connection. It takes its cues not from what we think about a situation, but from how it feels in our body right now.

The Nervous System Felt from Within

The nervous system isn't just a diagram in a textbook.

It's alive in you… weaving a tapestry between your body and mind with threads of living light.

It spreads out from your spine,

through your arms, into your fingertips,

into the soles of your feet, into your skin,

connecting every living cell.

It tells your whole being exactly what's happening in real time, filtered through your own unique perception of what feels safe and what doesn't.

The nervous system remembers everything. From the first cry to each sigh. It shapes how we experience being, and how we allow ourselves to become.

Each person's nervous system has its own exquisite form of intelligence, its own nature. For some, it moves like a hummingbird… quick, delicate, attuned to the environment. For others, it moves like a bear, slow to rise, deeply grounded in its inner safety. There are infinite expressions of sensitivity, awareness, and rhythm. All are sacred.

And what feels safe or threatening is deeply subjective. What feels completely normal and even fun for one person, like a rollercoaster ride or a scary movie, might overwhelm someone else entirely.

This is why so many misunderstandings arise: The world most of us live in today tends to favor fast-paced, high-stimulation environments. It naturally suits those whose systems thrive on speed, noise, and novelty. But not everyone is wired that way. Many people, young and old, need more quiet to connect with themselves.

Safety is not one-size-fits-all. And the more we understand this, the more power we have to meet it with care.

This Is What Safety Feels Like

Safety is not a rulebook. Not a locked door, or a well-lit hallway.
That's defense.

Safety is a nervous system exhale. A soul-sigh.
This moment when your body feels, "I have all I need."
And your heart says, "I can be exactly who I am… and it's safe to be myself here."

Safety isn't compliance. It isn't silence.
It isn't a child who looks well-behaved on the outside.

Safety is what allows life to happen. Not just survival, **life**.
Joy. Wonder. Curiosity. Mischief. Flow.

When a child feels safe, their mind opens.
Their eyes sparkle. They play, they wonder, they believe in themselves.
And we grown-ups, we need that too.
Every single one of us was once a child, looking for someone who would say,
"You are safe with me."

Some of us didn't get that. So now, we give it.
To ourselves. To our children. To each other.

Safety is not something you can talk anyone into.
It's something you carry like a lantern.
You offer it in the way you sit. The way you breathe. The way you listen.
And without saying a word, you tell the child beside you, and the child in you:

"You don't have to earn this.
You are already safe.
You are already loved."

We Are All Born Sensitive

All children are born with highly sensitive nervous systems. This is not a "flaw" of childhood; it's a biologically based trait with enormous strengths.
It is the wisdom of the body and the inner compass of each person.

This sensitivity is why children are the true masters of the Zone. While we adults are often lost in our schedules and worries, the child's nervous system is busy recording the shimmer of the light, the tone of our voice, and the feeling of the air. They are primed for presence because they cannot be anywhere else. Their bodies are vibrantly, sometimes painfully, awake to the current moment.

It's how they know when someone is safe,
how they seek comfort,
how they feel joy in the smallest leaf
or heartbreak in the faintest scolding.

A highly sensitive nervous system allows children to notice more, feel more,
and thus, learn more.

Children are often the ones who pick up on subtle cues, patterns, and relational dynamics that others might miss. This is emotional awareness as well as cognitive and intuitive intelligence. Their nervous systems are finely tuned to the environment. While this can be overwhelming in harsh conditions, it becomes a strength in nurturing settings.

Think of the young child who notices when their little sibling is upset before anyone else does. Maybe that was you. They speak in a softer voice, bring over a favorite toy, and instinctively create safety. That's a sensitive nervous system in action.

So often children speak up when something feels wrong, when a rule is unfair, or someone is left out. Their voice may tremble, but they can't stay silent. They carry an inner compass for justice. That's the sensitivity of conscience.

These are core strengths in a child's personality, and signs of a nervous system tuned not just to survive, but to sense, care, and respond with wisdom beyond their years.

Young children experience the world with an openness that many adults have gradually learned to filter out. Sounds, lights, emotions, and sensations arrive vividly and all at once, often filling their whole bodies. What we sometimes interpret as overreacting, defiance, or a tantrum can simply be a child trying to navigate a world that feels very big from the inside. The following words offer a glimpse into the inner experiences of a young child.

Inside My Big World

Inside my body, the world is big.
It hums and flashes and moves fast. Sometimes too fast.
Every sound is a visitor.
Every light is a question.
Every feeling lives in my whole body
not just in my heart.

You think I'm overreacting.
But I'm just reacting to everything...all at once.

When I cover my ears, it's not because I don't want to listen.
It's because I'm overwhelmed.
When I cry or push things away,
it's not out of spite.
It's because I don't know how to explain
that it's all too loud, too bright, too fast inside me.

You might see a tantrum.
I feel helpless and scared.

You might see defiance.
I feel paralyzed.

Sometimes you ask me to be okay with things that hurt me
because they don't hurt you.

Please know I'm not trying to give you a hard time. I'm having one.

But also...I notice the kindness in someone's eyes
before they even speak.

I feel music in my chest like a secret.
I see the color of the sky
when no one else is looking.

When someone speaks gently to me,
my whole body softens.

And when you join me in the Forever Now,
I don't feel so alone inside this big world.

Please don't just look at what I can't do.
See how much I'm already holding.
See how hard I'm trying to make sense of it all.

When I am met with tenderness,
I grow strong.

When I am given time,
I unfold.

And when I am allowed to be fully me,
I become the wonder
you hoped I would be.

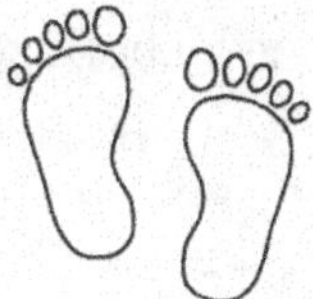

The Many Faces of Strength and Sensitivity

Some children are built with a more robust nervous system: bold, active, less visibly impacted by their surroundings. They may take the lead, charge forward, and learn best through movement and gross motor activities. This is also intelligence: the kind that thrives in motion, in risk-taking, in testing limits.

But it's important to remember: what appears strong on the outside isn't always the full story. Most robust-seeming children are deeply sensitive underneath. They simply cope in different ways. Humor, toughness, or constant motion can be their way of managing a world that often feels too much.

Sometimes the children who seem the strongest are the ones who feel the deepest. Their hearts may be just as tender, hidden beneath their brave faces, fast feet, or fearless voices.

From Vigilance to Presence

Every nervous system, whether child or adult, bold or sensitive, loud or quiet, is always doing the same essential thing: asking, "Is it safe to be here right now? Is it good for me to be here right now?"

Children are already in the Forever Now, but their sense of presence needs safety to deepen and flourish. And safety, for a child, lives in the adults around them. It deepens through the quality of attention an adult brings into the room.

The presence practices that follow are for both of you. When a grown-up settles into presence, a child feels it. You become the safety that opens their world. And in that opening, you both get to enjoy the Forever Now.

6

INVITATION 6
Tuning into the Forever Now

We don't experience the world through our eyes and senses alone, we experience it through our nervous system. The safer it feels, the more we can opens to the full texture of life. A tense nervous system walks through a garden and sees plants.
A settled one hears the rustle of leaves, catches the scent of soil after rain, notices the particular green of light through branches. And in that noticing, there is a sense of restoration.

The most nourishing thing available might not be far away in a retreat, a method, or a better version of yourself. It may be right here, in this ordinary moment, waiting to be noticed. When you let the mystery, the beauty, the sheer miracle of this moment fill you, something opens.

Your own wisdom surfaces. Learning becomes lighter.
Creativity arrives unexpectedly. And underneath all of it,
a growing sense that life, *as it is*, is enough right now.

The following practices are experiments...doorways to enter the Forever Now, for you and your child both. The moment you are already in *is* the portal.

Experiments for Tuning into the Forever Now

Here are a few simple experiments you can try right now and anytime in daily life. Try tuning into the Forever Now while waiting somewhere with your child, while preparing a meal, or while caring for your body. You may be surprised what the Forever Now reveals.

1. Learn Your Body's Language

Your body speaks to you through its needs. When you feel an inner "alarm" sounding, and you're stressed out, don't try to argue with it. Instead, start with the body. Offer it comfort. A glass of water. Eat something warm and nourishing. Step outside for a breath of fresh air. Nap if you can. These simple, earthy acts are how you say to your nervous system:

"It is safe to land in this moment."

"I can be with this and still be okay."

Notice what your body is asking for in this moment. It will bring you back.

2. Tune Into the Sounds of the Forever Now

Close your eyes for a moment and listen. What sounds are here, right now?

This is your audio backdrop of the Forever Now.

Is it the low hum of the fridge? Children's voices?

A car in the distance? Perhaps you hear birdsong, footsteps, or your own breath.

Let the soundscape wash over you.

You don't have to name or judge it.

Just notice. This moment is alive.

3. Notice the Play of Light and Shadow

The Forever Now is offering a light show to your eyes right now.

Begin by looking around and noticing the shadows in your room or outdoor space.

See the different shapes and subtle shades of gray and light that each object casts.

Watch how light and shadow shift and change the colors you see.

Perhaps you catch the way light rests in your child's hair, or how it dances across your hands as you move.

These small moments are always here, waiting to be seen.

Let yourself linger with this play of light and dark;

it's a simple way to tune into the Forever Now, wherever you are.

4. Look for Beauty in the Ordinary

Today, pick one simple task, like washing your hands, folding laundry, or preparing tea. Let your awareness rest with the process, follow it with all your senses.

If you're washing your hands, watch the way the water and soap swirl in perfect patterns, how the light catches each bubble.

If you're folding laundry, notice the warmth of the fabric,

the sound it makes as it's shaken out, the clean smells rising up.

If you're making tea, listen to the kettle, watch the steam curl, see the color slowly deepen in the cup.

Let it slow you down. Let it show you something new.

The ordinary is inviting you into the present.

5. Glow Up! Praise Yourself Lavishly

Whenever you feel insecure or out of sorts,

praise yourself for the smallest acts:

"Wow, I stirred that tea like a queen / a king."

"That was the most graceful door-closing in the history of ever."

"I breathed. I noticed. I came back. Well done, me."

The sillier the better. The more loving, the stronger the glow.

6. Let the Feelings Come With You

If messy emotions arise in you or your child as you become more present, it may mean your nervous system feels safe enough to bring something up for healing.

Every nervous system is shaped not only by what is happening *now*,
but also by everything you've lived and carried *before*.
Sometimes old experiences can appear as if they were current threats
and body and mind continue to brace as if that danger is still unfolding.

By bringing your attention back to what is actually here, you offer your body new information: there is no danger in this moment. You start feeling safe to let a wave of emotion move through, or you let your mind air out its charge, while you anchor in the safety of *here and now*.

Try saying inwardly: "It's safe to feel this. It is okay to think what I'm thinking.
I will keep breathing, keep anchoring in my Forever Now,
and keep taking care of myself and my child through all of it."

Presence is kindness. It's staying with yourself with compassion, with the child
beside you, with whatever the moment is offering, even if it's hard.
Especially then.

Over time, these experiments carve new pathways in your brain and relax your nervous system. Your mind begins to fully participate in the Forever Now, grounding you in the reality of your own life.

7

INVITATION 7

How Presence Changes the Mind

When you keep returning to the Forever Now, your personality begins to shift.
In this safety, higher capacities awaken...clarity, patience, and care.

You begin to recognize inner voices without obeying them, because you start
sensing that underneath the noise,
there's something much more tender going on...

Often we only notice the mind when it's loud and stressed.
We analyze it, try to control it, manage it, or escape it.
Some call it the ego and study it like detectives.

The mind is layered, like a whole inner family living in one house.
It holds the voice of the planner, the critic, the inner child, the protector...
every voice you've ever needed to survive.

It's everything you've lived through, and everything you're still healing.

But in the safety of the Forever Now, you start to realize, it's not your enemy;
it wants to be your friend.
Your mind is the most loyal, clever, loving protector you have.
It plans, solves, remembers, jokes, learns, dreams, and sometimes worries,
because it cares so much about keeping you safe, loved, and alive.
When your mind and nervous system feel truly safe in the present, the egoic

overly self-centered parts can relax. You can think of ego here as the way your nervous system learned early on "who I must be" in order to stay safe in the world. When that system feels held and no longer under constant threat, it shifts.

It stops defending, controlling, pleasing, or hiding.
It stops trying to be someone.
And instead… it becomes someone.

That's when ego steps into its healthy role: not as a defense system,
but as your personality, your radiant character, your you-ness.

You need an ego to move through the world. It gives you spunk,
style, perspective, and selfhood, your very own, unique identity structure.

A fearful mind keeps the ego tight and loud.
A clear, peaceful mind allows the ego to relax and shine.

And from that ease, a truer version of you gets to emerge:
more relaxed, more real, more responsive. This is the mind in flow with the heart:
anchored, discerning, awake. Less armor, more essence.

From here, often five main shifts appear that affect how and when you think:

Your Mind Becomes a Friend

A present mind begins to cooperate. It offers reminders of what matters, insights, and even humor. It no longer only scans for danger; it notices meaning, beauty, fun. The world feels more friendly, and your inner voice becomes kinder and wiser.

Your Mind Becomes a Super Learner

When defenses relax, curiosity returns. The mind starts asking real questions again. Learning no longer feels like pressure but like play. Suddenly, you find yourself captivated by history, karate, calligraphy, or Tibetan throat singing. Or inward, into learning about yourself, your inner life, your healing.
Curiosity leads, and the mind, feeling safe, says: "Yes, let's find out!"

Your Mind Becomes a Creator

Your imagination isn't some faraway dream machine...

it's the artist-in-residence of the Forever Now.

It's the inner sky of the present moment.

When you're imagining, you're not leaving reality.

You're making space for more of it to unfold.

You begin to sense new possibilities.

"What if?" becomes a doorway instead of a threat.

Even a bridge out of pain.

Because being present doesn't always mean being happy.

You can be grounded in the Forever Now, and still feel lost, lonely, or unwell.

That's why presence alone isn't always enough.

Sometimes, to stay with the moment, we need imagination to hold us.

Your Mind Becomes Still

Stillness isn't the absence of thought; it's the softening of the struggle.

The mind stops pushing, evaluating, or bracing.

It loosens its grip.

What remains is a gentle spaciousness, like the pause between waves.

In this quiet, you can hear yourself more clearly, not the anxious echoes,

but the truths underneath.

Life feels less like something to manage and more like something you can simply

meet, breath by breath.

Your Mind Enters the Zone More Easily

When we're in the Zone, something profound happens beneath the surface:

The busy council in our mind, the voices of doubt, fear, and protecting,

suddenly quiet, because something else takes the lead.

In flow, your very essence takes the wheel.

And when you lead from your most grounded self,

all the parts of you can exhale. For a moment, they feel safe.
Guided by a current stronger and wiser than any of them alone.

Flow is a state of unification.
All of you is still here, but harmonized, and swept up in a larger rhythm.

That current of energy moving through you,
teaches your mind something it never quite knew:

There is something inside you that knows what to do.
And it loves you enough to carry you.
You are not alone in yourself.

And when you come out of flow, something has changed.
Even if your mind returns with its usual noise and needs,
you've tasted safety.

You've seen what it's like to be carried.
And it begins to trust the deeper you,
the one who flows, the one who knows,
the one who leads with precision and love.

It's an Ongoing Process

As you keep returning to the Forever Now, these shifts don't arrive all at once,
and they rarely feel dramatic from the inside.
They show up in small, almost ordinary ways:
you hesitate before reacting,
you are kinder toward yourself after a mistake,
and you feel a flash of curiosity where there used to be dread.

Presence does not erase your history or your feelings,
but it changes the way you move with them.

It lets your whole inner world travel together,
more trusting, more coordinated, more free,
to meet the child in front of you,
and the life that is unfolding now.

Closing Reflection Part Two

Becoming present is the practice of a lifetime. Returning home to yourself happens again and again, in big and small ways, for yourself and together with children. And the more you practice, the more natural it feels. Over time, your simple presence becomes a place you trust.

And on this journey, our most eager teachers are already living right alongside us.

Children are the masters of learning and the undisputed champions of the Forever Now. As we move into the next part of our journey, we become full-hearted learners again.

Let's learn from children what they do so effortlessly and what we often forgot as we tried to find our footing in the adult world. It is time to rediscover the joy, the mess, and the fearless freedom of learning in flow like a child.

INVITATIONS IN THIS PART:

8 How Children Enter the Zone

9 Rediscover Flow Learning

∞ The Infinity Chapter

PART THREE

Learning Like a Child

What if the way children play is not a phase we grow out of, but a wisdom we are meant to grow back into?

Children are masters of flow. Their minds and hearts are still attuned to presence, wonder, and instinct. They follow joy without agenda, and they dive into life with all their senses open. In doing so, they show us what learning truly looks like when it's unburdened by pressure or praise. This is what I call Flow Learning.

This part of the book is a portal: an invitation to watch children closely, then turn inward and remember. You were once this alive, this curious, this able to lose yourself in something meaningful. You still are. Your mind, too, can come home to presence. Your body, too, can learn through play.

You don't need to become childlike...you already are under all the layers. Let's rediscover how we learn when nobody is watching. Let's reclaim the joy of learning like a child.

How Children Enter the Zone

Children are born masters of flow. For young children, being in the Zone is as natural as breathing. Their play unfolds in flow state because their brains are wired for presence.

They enter the Zone instinctively, as if it were the most natural thing in the world. Because for them, it is. Across continents, centuries, and cultures, children deliberately immerse themselves in their self-chosen activities. Flow is a universal language, a state every one of us experienced again and again in childhood and beyond.

Young children have fewer layers of judgment and mental noise, and more access to instinct, emotion, and direct sensory experience. This is because their prefrontal cortex is still developing well into adolescence. Where adults wrestle with overthinking, young children simply follow the thread of joy. This is why a child can disappear into play for thirty minutes, an hour, or sometimes longer.

As children grow, they develop more self-awareness, and often also more hesitation, doubts, and comparison. They might stay in a state of self-monitoring unless someone helps them drop in. This is where adult presence becomes essential. A tuned-in adult can offer not just materials or time, but also safety, encouragement, and a field of permission.

This Is First Flow Activity

Babies dwell in a continuous flow state, feeling one with all that is, and only slowly begin to learn about separation. They exist in a timeless, oceanic state of oneness with everything around them. Their first flow activities show them that they are a separate being, an individual who can cause things to happen. They are tiny, often missed or even found annoying, but they are the first signs of a child discovering themselves as an individual in relationship with the world. Here are examples of first flow activities:

Reaching to Grasp Something

That intense baby stretch for a toy just out of reach… the rolling, scooting, crawling that follows, these are our very first self-chosen challenges:

"Let's see if I can get there myself." If those early missions feel joyful, the brain says: More of this, please. If they don't, the brain might trim these impulses. This is where our lifelong relationship to movement begins, before we have words for it.

Throwing a Toy on the Floor

True, it can feel like: "Please, just stop dropping that toy!" But the baby is actually experimenting: "What happens if I do this? Will the world respond? Can I make something happen again?" That tiny drop-retrieve-drop loop is one of the origins of our drive for discovery, agency, and creative confidence. It's foundational for the inner drive behind creative activity.

The Deep Gaze

Have you ever noticed a baby staring with total intensity at a ceiling fan, a shadow, or, most powerfully, directly into your eyes? This gaze is a doorway to two different kinds of flow, depending on where they are looking:

Gazing to connect: When a baby locks eyes with you or follows a moving object, they are "zooming in." They are studying patterns, learning the geography of your face, and actually merging with you through their mirror neurons. This is the first flow state of connection and the beginning of "we."

Gazing into the void: When a baby stares at a blank wall or into the middle distance, they are often "zooming out." Because their world is a constant flood of new data, this is their biological pause button. It is a natural nervous system reset, a way to quiet the noise and give themselves a break inside. To an adult, it might look like they are "doing nothing." But in these moments, they are doing the most vital work of all: learning how to focus their attention to connect, and how to withdraw their attention to rest.

From the very beginning, our brain is pruning and shaping itself, strengthening the pathways that feel good, trimming the ones that don't. Those early moments already carry all the hallmarks of adult flow states.

The Unfolding of the Inner Self

As children transition from toddlers into young explorers, flow activities become more complex and multilayered. They are no longer just exploring the physics of throwing a spoon, but the architecture of their own minds.

There is an old wisdom that says we only truly reveal ourselves when we play. In the Zone, the "armor" of the world drops away, and a child's true individuality begins to shine through. You see it in the way one child builds a city with meticulous order, while another creates a wild world of chaos and story.

In an environment that protects their focus and honors their pace, children don't outgrow flow; they grow into it.

In the next pages, let's step inside the body of a five-year-old and a ten-year-old in flow and feel what it's like for a children to be thriving in the Zone.

Inside the Body of a 5-Year-Old in Flow

Inside my body, it feels like I'm flying, but I'm barely moving.
It feels like my feet are on the floor, but the floor is part of a story,
and the story is moving me.

One eye sees what's really there... a spoon, a block, a crumb
and the other eye sees what's really real:
a spaceship, a mountain,
a tiny world waiting to be built.

Every building block I place has a purpose.
It becomes a little farm, or a firefighter station.
Every drawing I make carries an intention:
To help my mom and dad get along.
To bring that butterfly to life on the page.
To say something with my heart when I don't yet have the words.

And when I do it, I feel cozy and warm inside.
Like there's harmony between my inside and the outside.
The world I create reflects the world I long for.
And in that world, I am completely safe.

I play until I feel safe.
I build until I feel proud.
I draw until it feels complete.
That's how I know I'm done.

When I'm in this place, I don't hear you calling right away.
I don't feel time the same.
It's like time becomes golden and stretchy.

I don't even know I have a body,
I am the game, the building,
the song, the swirl of water, the shadow on the floor.
I am what I'm doing.

The world disappears. The world appears.
And I am the one who gets to make it.

Everything inside me is whole and complete.
And in that wholeness, I discover who I am
and become who I'm meant to be.

Flow Creates a Map of Inner Strength

Childhood flow state is a map of inner strength being formed. When a child learns through their own play that they can shape the world around them, when they experience safety, joy, and pride from their own hands, from their own ideas, they are building inner resources that will support them for life.

This is how children build resilience: not by being told to "be strong," but by feeling strong in the sanctuary of their own creations.

In the Zone, they're in dialogue with the world... testing, shaping, responding, receiving. But it's not just about learning new facts; it's the whole body, whole being experience of bringing meaning to their world in the most joyful way possible.

Through these self-chosen moments, children aren't just gathering knowledge, they're shaping their personalities, forming their identities, and discovering what lights them up inside. They're discovering, through lived experience:

"I can shape my environment."
"The world responds to me."
"I know how to move forward."

Older children choose ever more intricate, inventive, and layered projects. Their bodies are larger, their hands more capable, and their imagination more expansive. The inner current of curiosity is still the same, but now it moves through more complex tools, ideas, and self-chosen challenges. Flow becomes a creative force, shaping a child's world from the inside out.

Let's step into the body of a ten-year-old, mid-flow, and see what this kind of learning looks like from the inside.

Inside the Body of a 10-Year-Old Who Builds a Robot from Boxes

It begins with an image, a flash of vision.
It lives in the hands.
It's an ache to make something real.

I scan the room. My inner spark is already dancing ahead,
pulling the body with it.

Cardboard, scissors, markers, tape.
Nothing is planned. Everything is known.

Inside my body, there's a buzz. Like a light turning on behind my ribs.
My fingers tingle with ideas, they already know what to do:

The big box becomes the chest.

The cereal box is for the head.

Toilet paper rolls? Arms, of course.

Each piece finds its place like magic.

It's not just a robot. It's my robot.

It has a name. A mission. A heart made of tinfoil.

When I tape the legs just right, I feel strong.

When I cut out the eyes, I feel smart.

When I paint the buttons, I feel like I'm building something real,

something that matters.

I'm not just making... I'm becoming.

An inventor. A creator.

Someone who can take a pile of recycling

and turn it into a friend.

Time folds up like paper.

My feet forget to wiggle.

My snack gets cold. And I don't mind at all.

There's no right or wrong here.

Only "yes." Only "this."

Only "more tape, please."

The robot is standing now.

I step back.

We look at each other.

And something inside me smiles.

I made this. I did this.

And for a little while,

the world and I were building each other.

Children are never "just playing;" they're practicing agency. They're learning that their ideas matter, that their hands can shape reality, and that they can bring something into existence that wasn't there before. Creative flow becomes a rehearsal space for life: a place where mistakes don't feel dangerous, where starting over is part of the adventure, and where pride comes from within rather than from praise.

Sometimes children will even scare themselves on purpose as part of play. They might hide, jump out, roar like monsters, or pretend to be frightened while laughing at the same time. This kind of playful excitement is very different from real fear; it is a form of safe thrill that children explore because it feels energizing and fun.

In a similar way, many children enjoy *play fighting* or *dramatic action play*. They may be acting out scenes they've seen in stories or movies, repeating them until the experience feels familiar and safe. For some children it can also express natural archetypal energies such as the hunter, the protector, or the warrior. When this kind of imaginative play happens within clear, safe boundaries (when no one gets hurt, everyone participates willingly, and other children's comfort is respected) then it is a normal and healthy part of development.

A child who experiences this kind of self-generated inner peace carries that strength into friendships, schoolwork, challenges, and eventually into adulthood. However, this kind of confidence doesn't bloom in isolation. It needs a sense of safety that only an adult can offer.

One Safe Grown-Up is Needed

Children enter the Zone most easily when their environment invites them to explore, when their genuine needs are met, and when they feel emotionally safe.

Emotional safety is most reliably provided by a trusted adult. While peers may offer companionship and play, they cannot offer deep reassurance, because they, too, are looking for it.

Neuroscience shows that already in infancy, a child's nervous system attunes to their caregivers. As they grow up, children seek safe adults for co-regulation and permission to focus on their play. When the adult slows down and is kind, they settle and feel safe enough to explore.

Over time, as children grow into teenagers, they integrate the repeated experience of being met and form secure attachment patterns within themselves. They learn to regulate themselves even when a safe adult is not right there. This inner safety supports them as they step into the wider world. Our culture rarely teaches a child to look within. It teaches them to chase approval, and to seek fulfillment in praise, image, and productivity. It teaches them that who they are is not enough unless someone else says so.

With your presence, you can send a different message:
"There's something inside you that's worth following."
"Some answers can only be found within."
"You can trust yourself."
"There's joy in making, doing, exploring for yourself, not just for others."

Even if a child doesn't understand these words yet, they feel them. And that feeling becomes an inner compass. Even if they lose their way later (as most of us do) they'll remember. Somewhere deep inside, they'll know they can come back to themselves.
Because someone once believed in them.

Here, you might be wondering: *But is this really how my child learns?*
What if I don't see this happening?
What if I'm not sure how to support it... or if I'm even the right person to try?

These questions matter because while Flow Learning is natural, it isn't automatic. In Part Four we'll explore how to become that steady presence for the children in your life. And in Part Five, we'll journey inward to reaffirm that presence for yourself.

Start Watching for Flow in Children

Children enter the Zone whenever they have an opportunity, especially in the early years. With warmth and support, this capacity stays alive and can be carried forward into adulthood.

Flow in children shares nearly all the same markers as adult flow, with one radiant difference: imagination takes center stage. A child's self-led play introduces elements of symbolic thinking and pretend scenarios that adults rarely use during their flow activities.

Another marker to be aware of is a child's eager repetition of things they already know, such as stories, movements, songs, puzzles, or hands-on creations. This is an early form of self-motivated practice and one of the roots of self-discipline.

When children are in the Zone, they are especially open and receptive. The words we speak in those moments can become part of the voice they carry inside themselves later in life. A simple encouragement like "You did great," "I love how you're figuring that out," or "Keep going, I know you can do it" may one day echo within them as their own inner support.

Here Are Some Signs That Show a Child in the Zone:

- The child is deeply absorbed; there is no doubt this is what they want to do.
- They start where they feel safe and stretch as they go, balancing skill with novelty.
- They stay curious, experiment, and repeat what they've learned.
- They don't worry about "getting it right."
- They may forget time, hunger, or bathroom breaks.
- Imagination, pretend, and role play often lead the way.

These markers signal a child who is fully alive in the moment, building the invisible foundation for a lifetime of access to the Zone.

How Can You Tell a Child Was Just in the Zone?

You can see it in the way they carry themselves as they "surface" back into the room. Their eyes have a specific kind of shine, not the frantic sparkle of overstimulation, but a steady, quiet glow. Their smile comes from deep inside.

In these moments, they aren't looking to you for a "Good job!" or a gold star. They aren't seeking approval; they are already happy. You don't have to do anything; you simply get to join them in their happiness.

They seem more settled in their skin, more anchored in their own spirit, because they have just fed their soul.

Helping Children Transition Out of Flow

When it's time to close a flow activity, remember that a child may not respond to your voice right away. This isn't defiance; it is deep immersion. They are quite literally in another world.

To honor this focus and preserve your connection, move into their space slowly. Instead of calling from across the room, come close. Gently touch their shoulder or arm to ground them, say their name softly, and wait. Give them the "buffer time" they need to bridge the gap between their inner world and the outer one. Wait until their eyes meet yours.

Acknowledge the beauty of what they were doing:

"I can see how deeply you were just in that world. It's hard to pull away when your heart is so full of what you're making."

Since flow can carry children (and grown-ups) so far that they lose track of their own bodies, use gentle external anchors like soft timers or a "five-minute song."

This helps them land softly, ensuring they don't feel "snapped" out of their joy, but rather guided back home to the next moment.

Flow *Is* the Practice

Flow is a habit of the body, brain, and nervous system, and childhood is the perfect time to build it. Every time a child becomes absorbed in play, they carve neural pathways that make it easier to return to the Zone again and again, also as adults.

This is why creative play in childhood is so powerful: it lays down the living tracks of presence. It teaches the whole being how to come home to the moment, effortlessly, joyfully, and for life.

And when adults engage their hands, hearts, and full attention in a creative task, they, too, awaken those tracks. Flow isn't just for small tasks; it's how we build trust in ourselves to take on bigger things, too. Flow is the practice. It's how we learn, how we heal, and how we rediscover who we are, at any age.

Let's take a closer look at this natural intelligence.
Let's rediscover Flow Learning.

9

INVITATION 9

Rediscover Flow Learning

This invitation is for you: This is a journey through your most authentic mind. It's about what you might remember from your childhood, or perhaps you never forgot...

Flow Learning is not a method; it's a return to the way you once learned, before anyone told you how learning was supposed to look. It's a reawakening to the part of you that explored, created, played, and discovered without pressure or comparison. That part of you is still here.

When you learn something truly important to you such as how to care for a plant, how to speak your truth, or how to center yourself, you don't just gain information. You become more whole. More capable. More you.

Flow Learning is what happens when learning moves from the head into the hands and heart. When you follow a thread of curiosity until it becomes a current of transformation.

So take a breath and put on your explorer's hat.
We're heading into the wild, alive territory of lifelong learning.

When Learning Lives in the Body

We often think of learning as an intellectual pursuit. But the most natural kind of learning, the kind young children do all the time, is full-bodied and full-hearted. It includes your hands and body, movement, emotion, rhythm, repetition, and play. It's deeply personal and completely alive.

This kind of learning happens when something matters to you. It might be how to prepare food, organize your space, style your hair, build a ramp, or speak in public. It might come through pleasure and play: dancing, skiing, drawing, or drumming. And it might emerge in your work, your calling, or your healing journey.

And here's the most important part: Flow Learning is about your *own* joy, your *own* aliveness, and your *own* curiosity.

Your child might want to join you, which would be wonderful. Or they will find another activity that lights them up in the moment. Perhaps they prefer to play nearby in their own world, that's great too. You're both immersed in presence, and that's what matters most.

When *you* love what you're doing, you are building an inner resource: Flow activities make you not only smarter, but wiser, more adaptable, and more creative.

Flow Learning shapes you: it changes your posture, your voice, your sense of what matters. It helps you shed what no longer fits and reach for what truly calls you. It's the difference between living someone else's story and finding your own.

And in doing so, you show your child that it's okay to create joy for yourself.

Learning How To Learn

When children enter the flow state, they practice how to learn. Not with step-by-step instructions or formal lessons. Not even with the label "learning" attached.

Children often start at a point where they already know something, where they feel comfortable enough to explore. And because of that, it doesn't feel like learning. It feels like playing. And you can do that, too!

Underneath, pure magic is at work. You are rediscovering the inner workings of learning...how to feel safe following your curiosity, how to build on what you know, and how to adjust when things don't go as planned.

There's a saying in jazz: "It's not the note you play that's the wrong note. It's the note you play afterwards that makes it right or wrong." We all make mistakes. We miss a beat. We lose our way. But what matters is the note we play next: how we respond, how we recover, how we move forward. When a child experiences this early on, they keep trusting the process. Mistakes become bridges, not dead ends.

A young violinist scratches out their first notes, not for a gold star, but because something deep inside wants to make music. When learning feels safe, even the discomfort feels different, like stretching into something you already love.

We can learn this from children. They are self-guided, but even that term doesn't quite capture the magic... it's like the activity itself is pulling them forward. It's alive. It's moving. It's inviting them to keep playing.

In these moments, children aren't focused on outcomes or approval. They're simply engaged. Fully, deeply, and joyfully. And this is where some of the most profound learning takes place, the kind that can't be measured, the kind that becomes part of them.

This is where children develop a relationship with learning itself. Where learning becomes a friend and a forever companion.

Revisiting Childhood Learning

So many of us grew up experiencing learning as something we have to rush through, where you try to get everything right, meet expectations, and keep up with everyone else.

But Flow Learning is different.
It doesn't demand that you hurry.
It welcomes your full attention and lets you go at your own pace.

You don't need to compete or compare.
You're not trying to impress anyone.
You're simply allowing yourself (or your child) to enjoy the process of learning.

You'll hit bumps. You'll feel awkward.
You'll hear the old voices that say, "I'm not good at this."

But this time, you'll breathe. You'll keep going.
You'll offer yourself the kindness you needed as a child.
And you'll teach your whole system: Learning is safe.
Mistakes are okay. You can trust your pace.

Flow Learning is a return to joy, and to your own power.
It invites you to notice the little things: the way your hands move,
the sounds around you, the spark of curiosity as you try something new.

Each moment becomes an invitation to slow down,
savor, and rediscover the wonder of your creativity.
And with each step, you're not just learning a skill,
you're becoming someone who trusts their own process.

Start With Tinkering

Learning something new rewires your brain in the best way, at any age. But starting something big, like learning Tibetan or the cello, might feel like a lot right now, and that's okay. You don't have to climb a mountain to rewire your brain. Even just tinkering can make a huge difference.

You can start with the simplest thing that's fun for you. For instance, I love doing jigsaw puzzles, because puzzles welcome everyone. Someone can join or leave at any time, without breaking the flow. And here's what I learn every time I sit down to do one: It takes patience. You can try a piece in the wrong place for as long as you like...it won't fit. It only fits where it truly belongs.

And most of all, puzzles tend to free my mind. Instead of looping thoughts, my awareness moves into my hands, into color, shape, and patterns.
My breath slows. I start to see again, not just look.
Something comes together in real time, right under my fingertips.
It's satisfying and uplifting.

These small, playful moments awaken the learning circuits.
They invite the brain to open up to novelty, and they invite the body to relax into learning without pressure.

And maybe, for you, that's the real challenge. Because maybe you're used to chasing big goals, pushing hard, proving yourself. Maybe what feels uncomfortable now isn't the big effort, but doing something just for the joy of it. Without a purpose or a goal. Without needing the drawing to be beautiful or the pencil holder to stand up straight.

Just watching your own hands doing silly things that don't make sense.

Just sitting beside your child and smiling.

Just letting the moment be enough.

And you know what? That's perfect.

Because what you're really doing is creating new pathways that tell your nervous system: "You're safe here. Learning can feel good.
You can play. You can take your time."
This the deepest kind of learning and it will propel you forward in anything you'd like to achieve.

Learning Something Big in a Playful, Relaxed Way

You're an adult now. You decide to learn how to snowboard. You don't know how. You keep falling, your body aches, and it feels wildly uncomfortable. But because you've learned how to learn at the tinkering table, you don't panic or freeze. Instead, you get curious. You keep practicing. You adjust your stance. You try again. You keep playing, because you know this is part of the process.

Or maybe you decide to learn to speak in public, and you dedicated time to practice every week. You've never done it before, and your hands are shaking. But you don't give up. You tinker with your delivery. You trust that you'll figure it out. You follow your intuition, you experiment, and you keep going. Because you know now that's part of the process. You've practiced this. You've built a friendship with learning.

And here's the most beautiful part: When life hands you something really hard such as a career change, a big move, or a relationship that's falling apart, you don't collapse. You bring that same flexible, curious, self-trusting energy. You know you can try, make mistakes, find the next step, and keep playing and feeling your way forward.

This is the true gift of Flow Learning...it builds the inner strength that says,
"I may not know what comes next, but I keep going.
I will learn what I need to learn and I will grow and heal along the way."

~ *Fun Activities to Start Flow Learning*

Flow Learning begins with trying something new. Each of these activities is self-contained, learnable, and flow-friendly. Choose one thing and dive in, side by side with your child, or all on your own:

- ~ Try juggling three balls (or start with two)

- ~ Make a pencil holder out of cardboard, clay, or wood

- ~ Learn to play a song on the piano, ukulele, or recorder

- ~ Try calligraphy with a real ink pen

- ~ Learn to identify the trees in your yard or neighborhood

- ~ Build a kite and fly it

- ~ Make a marble maze from recycled materials

- ~ Craft your own earrings

- ~ Film your own stop-motion animation with toys

- ~ Learn to tie knots or basic sewing stitches

- ~ Learn to read a compass and make a mini map

- ~ Try shadow puppetry with a flashlight and cardboard cutouts

Trying even one of these, you might just discover how fun learning can be, no matter how old you are.

Once you begin, you may notice a rhythm and a natural sequence that flow learning tends to follow. It's how you know you're on the right path, even when the first challenges arise. Let's take a closer look at that progression. Let's take a closer look at that progression in the next pages.

Flow Learning Follows a Rhythm

Flow Learning follows a rhythm…a movement from hesitation, to engagement, to challenge, and into deep focus and joy.

Here's what this process often looks like:

1. The Challenge of Getting Started
2. Finding the Next Small Step
3. The Zigzag of Flow Learning
4. Healthy Focus
5. The Flow Lift: Now You're in the Zone
6. After the Flow: What Remains

1. The Challenge of Getting Started

When you catch a glimpse of someone doing something interesting, perhaps you wonder, *Could I try that, too?* But every new activity has a gatekeeper that asks, "Are you curious enough to stay, even if it feels awkward at first, even if you think you can't do it?" Before we find our rhythm in a new skill, we usually wobble through uncertainty and take a few clumsy steps. Toddlers show us this instinctively. They fall, rise, and try again, propelled by the simple desire to learn. As adults, we can borrow that courage and combine it with our lived wisdom.

2. Finding the Next Small Step

Frustration is part of flow. Whether you're building something, practicing an instrument, or writing a book, there comes a moment when doubt appears and the next step isn't clear.

Instead of pushing to finish, you can ask questions like: "What's the next joyful small step?" "Do I need a tool, a break, or support from another person?" Often, one small shift opens the next door. And the joy of overcoming a challenge is one of the most empowering experiences we know.

3. The Zigzag of Flow Learning

Flow Learning moves between stillness and motion, action and reflection. One moment you're absorbed, the next you pause to stretch or look out the window. This is not distraction but recalibration.

You might start planting seeds, then decide to label them first, then water one row before finishing the bed. The work unfolds in its own rhythm. Children craft and play this way naturally, and many adults do too when pressure is removed.

Accepting this zigzag can be a relief for anyone who struggles with straight-line focus. Learning does not always move from A to B. Some of us take the scenic route.

4. Healthy Focus or Hyperfocus?

Deep engagement is sometimes mistaken for hyperfocus. But when an activity is hands-on and meaningful, long attention can be a sign of health rather than a problem. Instead of measuring time, look for clues: Is the activity self-driven? Does it support the body and sense of identity? Will this be remembered as a time of trust and pride?

These are signs of thriving in flow. What may not look productive on the surface is shaping the inner architecture of a life.

5. The Flow Lift: Now You're in the Zone

Then at some point comes the shift into flow…it's like you're lifted: breath slows, shoulders soften, and you simply, effortlessly do, create, play, move, talk with a fluidity that feels just right.

Nothing outside changed, yet everything inside did. You arrived fully in what you're doing, enjoying the uplifting energy of the Zone.

You might find yourself drifting in and out, fluctuating between conscious effort and flow taking over. At first a few minutes in conscious effort, and then a few in flow again and so on. That's common.

With practice, though, you'll stay longer. And eventually, you won't be thinking about it at all. You'll just keep playing, simply enjoying the feeling of being carried by the activity itself.

Again and again, you'll surprise yourself with what you're capable of and what actually emerges: a new melody, a different recipe, a never-before-seen poem. Sometimes you begin shaping a vase and by the end that same lump of clay has become a soup bowl with googly eyes. The outcome may change, but the current of joy stays the same.

Bonus Tip: Find simple things that help you shift into flow: a favorite pen, a special playlist, comfortable clothes, or a place that feels good. These cues signal the nervous system: it's time to enter the Zone.

And slowly it all makes sense...the point of flow learning isn't to get perfect at something; it's to enjoy the process. And when you enjoy something, you do get better, naturally, over time, as you keep showing up for what you love.

6. After the Flow: What Remains

And then, as unexpectedly as it arrived, the moment shifts again.
Life as usual resumes.
The phone rings. Someone calls your name. Dinner needs to be made.

Maybe you and/or your child made something you love. Maybe it ended in a glorious mess. Maybe you didn't "finish" at all, but something inside you changed along the way.

Every hands-on activity reshapes the mind. When you use your hands and body with that much care new neural pathways form and you hone your capacity to flow with presence in whatever you do.

This is why doing matters. The activity may look simple, but something deep is happening. Mind and body learn together, and you emerge more open, more flexible, and more ready for what comes next.

Flow Learning Leads to Genuine Intelligence

There are over 8 billion people on Earth
and yet, no one is exactly like you or your child.
Each of us carries a unique world inside,
a secret realm of thoughts, ideas, and ways of seeing life.
Your inner world holds gifts *only you* can offer.

Flow learning leads straight to your most genuine expression of intelligence because it's the direct path to your unique way of seeing the world.

Your intelligence is not only the storage room of facts in your mind, even though tapping into that can be useful at times. Most importantly, your intelligence is a living current you tune into when you let life touch you.

It so often begins with a fearless question… not one we rush to answer, but one we dare to live with. Stay with a question long enough, and insights arrive over time.

This kind of intelligence asks for the sensitivity, curiosity, and courage you experience in Flow Learning. It asks that you let your environment, the materials you're studying, the people around you, and even silence keep informing you.

Over time, answers spiral: what you grasp at age ten returns at fifteen or fifty, each time revealing new layers because you have grown.

Your Unique Flavor of Intelligence

Harvard psychologist Howard Gardner introduced the Theory of Multiple Intelligences to show that there are many ways to be smart. He named nine distinct types of intelligence, doorways to understanding our unique minds.

Every child and adult holds many of these intelligences, and many more in different combinations. The more we recognize and nurture them, the more each person can thrive in their own way.

As you read through the list of these intelligences, think of yourself and your child: What excites you? What lights them up? What could you explore together?

1 Verbal-Linguistic Intelligence

Linguistic intelligence lives in language: speaking, writing, reading, and storytelling. It shines in those who love to play with language, express ideas clearly, and communicate through conversation or writing.

2 Logical- Mathematical Intelligence

This intelligence involves logic, patterns, and problem-solving. It shows up in puzzles, strategy games, and real-life math like measuring cooking ingredients or sorting toys.

3 Spatial-Visual Intelligence

Spatial thinkers visualize shapes and spaces. Artists, designers, and builders often use it when imagining or creating something in 3D.

4 Bodily-Kinesthetic Intelligence

This is the intelligence of movement. Dancers, athletes, craftspeople, and children all use their hands and bodies to explore, learn, and express.

5 Musical Intelligence

Musical intelligence is the gift of rhythm, melody, and harmony. It lives in those who whistle, hum, sing, play instruments, or deeply feel music.

6 Interpersonal Intelligence

People with this intelligence are skilled at reading emotions, collaborating, and building relationships. It shows in leaders, friends, and peacemakers.

7 Intrapersonal Intelligence

This is the ability to understand yourself, your feelings, values, and motivations.

8 Naturalist Intelligence

This intelligence connects us to the living world, the plants, animals, weather, and ecosystems. Nature lovers, gardeners, and young explorers often show this strength.

9 Existential Intelligence

Existential thinkers wonder about life's big questions: why we're here, what matters, what lies beyond. This intelligence seeks meaning and purpose.

More Ways to Be Brilliant

Spending time in *flow learning environments*, I've noticed many more kinds of intelligence that often come alive in children, teenagers, and grown-ups who are free to follow their curiosity and learn in flow. Here are some that stand out.

Visionary Intelligence

This is our imagination. Visionaries imagine what does not yet exist. They invent, create, and dream up bold new possibilities.

Practical Intelligence

This is hands-on smarts: making things work, solving real-world problems, and fixing what's broken.

Empathic Intelligence

This is the capacity to feel what others feel, and to bring warmth and care into relationships.

Highly Sensitive Intelligence

High sensitivity is the intelligence that picks up on subtle details, such as sounds, facial expressions, shifts in mood or energy. This intelligence can lead to great insight and creativity when paired with rest and support.

And Flow State is the Master Key

Flow opens the door to our particular blend of intelligences so we can learn, create, relate, and live from who we really are.

Which ways of thinking feel most alive in your child? Which ones feel alive in you? Have fun exploring how brilliant you already are!

The Magic You've Always Known

So many kinds of intelligence come alive through flow in movement, music, language, empathy, invention... but one often slips under the radar... it's playful, it's peculiar, and it just might be the most powerful one of all:
the intelligence of absurdity.

Just when you think you've got it all figured out...your multiple intelligences lined up neatly, your ducks marching in perfect rows, usually something unexpected slips in and rearranges everything!

Welcome to a surprise chapter that sneaks in next: The Infinity Chapter

It's here to remind you that flow transcends ordinary life and leads us straight to awe and wonder.

Have a slice of infinity pie!

SURPRISE!

∞ THE INFINITY CHAPTER ∞

Embracing the Intelligence of Absurdity

***Why the Infinity Chapter? Because this chapter isn't quite like the others.
It slipped in sideways when no one was looking...like the cutest little glitter-covered raccoon sneaking into a tea party.***

Absurdity is a missing piece of how we understand learning and intelligence, and it shares something essential with infinity: both puzzle the mind. Both interrupt the tidy logic of our lives and make us pause, tilt our head, and feel awe...
and that's when the unknown slips in and expands our sense of what's possible.

When something feels absurd, it often means you're stepping beyond what your mind (your default mode network) was trained to accept. And that's where some of the most beautiful, world-changing ideas are born...
Washing hands because of invisible bacteria? Absurd, so it seemed in 1847!
Talking to anyone in the world instantly? Whole libraries and all the music in the world in our pockets? Impossible, until suddenly they weren't.

When we shun absurdity, we risk closing off an entire dimension of creative intelligence. But when we lean in, we unlock play, flexibility, and flow.

Children still feel comfortable in worlds where nothing needs to make sense.
They aren't waiting for life to be orderly, they're busy living it.

Adults often rush to correct them, to return them to "normal," but these moments are not distractions from learning, they are the neural pathways of adaptability and creativity in formation. When we join them, we step into a magical playground for the mind.

The Secret Weapon of Geniuses, Comedians and Cultural Icons

Absurdity tickles the imagination and reminds us that life is more than what we can measure. Some of the brightest minds thrived on nonsense and imaginative leaps. Albert Einstein imagined riding on a beam of light. This idea helped give rise to the theory of relativity and forever changed how we understand time, space, and our place in the universe.

Charlie Chaplin, in the midst of the Great Depression, brought lightness to heavy times by famously dancing with dinner rolls and reminding people of the healing power of laughter.

Salvador Dalí painted melting clocks, giving form to the fluid, dreamlike nature of time and the unconscious. Dr. Seuss famously said, "I like nonsense, it wakes up the brain cells." All of them showed us that nonsense can be genius in disguise.

Others followed ideas that seemed absurd in their time. Visionaries like Galileo Galilei, Thomas Edison, Nikola Tesla, and Buckminster Fuller reshaped the world with their fearless thought experiments—and great minds still do today.

A Signal of Fearlessness

Absurdity sends a powerful message to the nervous system:
I'm not afraid. I'm not rushing. I have time for fun.

Imagine two sheep competing in a boredom contest. One stares at a rock for fifteen minutes. The other whispers, "Whoa... he's on fire." The second sheep nods solemnly: "Legend."

When we allow ourselves to be absurd, to say weird things, to play without purpose, and to giggle for no reason, we declare within ourselves: It's safe to step outside the known.

Many people fear what they don't understand. But when we let ourselves play in absurdity, we train our minds to feel safe in the unknown. We practice being at peace with what cannot be controlled or neatly explained.

Absurdity welcomes us into the grand mystery of life, and invites us to say YES.

Shortcut to Flow

Flow loves a little nonsense. It appears the moment you loosen your grip. When you chase a rubber duck across a puddle just to see where it goes.

Yes, the shortest distance between two dots is a straight line.

But flow doesn't care about straight lines.

Flow loops and wiggles, hops on one foot, and somehow arrives first.

Absurdity is a wormhole. A hidden shortcut that only appears when you stop trying to make sense.

When you yawn dramatically, sing in the shower instead of forcing the next step, or balance a spoon on your nose, flow often slips in, like a cat jumping onto your lap, and delivers the answer.

Sometimes that answer arrives as synchronicity, sometimes as a happy accident, sometimes as a small treasure you didn't even know you were seeking.

Absurdity fools the brain into letting go. And every so often, it opens hidden portals to ideas you could never have reached through logic alone.

The Logic of Absurdity

Absurdity has its own logic, and it rarely obeys the rules of efficiency or productivity. It's not about ticking off boxes or climbing the mountain of achievement.

It follows the logic of wonder and awe: the delight of slowing down enough to notice the marvelous in the mundane, the mischief that arises when we say yes to nonsense for no reason except joy.

It fuels a thousand small rebellions against boredom and drudgery. It gives us permission to break character in the play of life.

Absurdity says: "Delight yourself, even if no one sees. Make beauty, even if it lasts just a second. Talk to the world, and it might just talk back."

It's a different kind of logic altogether, the kind that declares,
"Everything is alive. Everything is waiting to play with you."

This is the logic that children know instinctively and adults can rediscover... sometimes with the help of a toddler or the discovery of their Inner Child.

Children Don't Make Sense
and That's the Magic

Young children cry when you peel a banana the "wrong" way.
They talk to stuffed animals like old friends.
They wear pajamas as superhero capes and won't step on tiles
because "the floor is lava."

To adults, this seems illogical. But to a child, it makes perfect sense.

They follow the logic of how it feels,
how it sounds in their imagination,
how it fits in the story they've already told themselves.

That banana had a backstory. That stuffed animal is real.
That upside-down view under the table is a whole new world.

They are not only pretending, they are participating in a world that is alive, interconnected, and fully real to them.

They move according to the logic of connection,
the logic of delight,
and the logic of play.

They are not trying to make sense in the adult world.
They are building one that makes sense to them.

They teach us to slow down for beauty.
To follow what's funny, what feels right, what glows.

When we slow down and meet them in their world,
that's when true connection begins.

So the next time you hear a child say "jamma winniebinnie boobidoo,"
or invent a game that makes absolutely no sense, smile.
You may be witnessing genius in one of its earliest, purest forms.

~ *Ring-a-ding-ding! Your Inner Fool Wants to Play* ~

Even if you were told as a child, "Stop that nonsense. Don't be silly," you can bring your inner fool back to life. And I mean fool in the most loving way: a person who isn't afraid to play with abandon, to make no sense at all, and to delight in it. Here are a few quick ways to wake them up:

1. Pretend you're visitors from another planet and don't know anything about this place.

2. Speak fluent gibberish. For five minutes, have a conversation in a made-up language. Shoobidee mammady runnabee? Absolutely. Notice how your body feels when it's free to play with sound and nonsense.

3. Give Everyday Objects Secret Identities: Your mug is now "Lord Earl of Steepington." The houseplant is the local weather forecaster. Narrate their adventures as you go about your day.

Each small act of playful absurdity is a love letter to life itself, a reminder that joy is a skill and nonsense is an ancient medicine. The more you welcome your inner fool, the more you invite flow, laughter, and creative magic into your world.

The Art of Switching Between Logics

Rational thinking and taking care of what must be done is important, no doubt. But that kind of logic is only one instrument in life's orchestra. Living well means learning to play by ear as much as by the sheet.

Sometimes life invites you to wander, to walk the extra mile, or to laugh when you spill the milk. These moments are invitations to let go of the map and be present with what is. The art is knowing when to switch. The more logics you can dance between, the richer life becomes. A world of color, not just black and white.

You might be stuck in efficiency mode if you're rushing for no reason or find it hard to play, slow down, and breathe. To shift the vibe do something deliciously unnecessary. Go outside and watch the clouds. Doodle. Make a silly face at your reflection. Remind yourself: "I am not a machine. I am allowed to be beautifully inefficient sometimes."

And sometimes you might be stuck in absurdity mode, for instance when you avoid practical tasks that matter or float without ever quite landing. To shift the vibe complete one small, concrete task. Fold a towel. Make your bed. Pay a bill. Notice how a simple act of completion brings a sense of satisfaction and helps play feel safer.

Life is part checklist, part confetti parade, a wild and wonderful mix of order and magic, discipline and delight.

Switching logics is a superpower. It keeps life fresh, joyful, grounded, and real.
You can move. You can play.
You can complete. You can rest.
And, you can always start again.

Because the best lives aren't lived in either/or. They're lived in between getting things done, and letting yourself be undone by beauty and fun.

A Completely Playful, Totally Unscientific Quiz

What Logic Are You In When You're With a Child Today:

Efficiency Mode or Play Mode?

Let's find out how you're dancing with life (and small humans) today! No need to take it seriously... just follow the giggles.

1. A child insists their stuffed animal has a stomach ache. What do you do?

> A) Quickly offer to "fix it" so you can move on to the next thing.
>
> B) Prepare an imaginary tea and ask what the stuffed animal would like to eat.
>
> C) Declare a city-wide stuffed animal medical emergency and start making siren noises.

2. A child wants to put socks on their hands and pretend to be a dinosaur. What's your move?

> A) You suggest it's not practical and help them put the socks on their feet.
>
> B) You put your socks on your hands and start crawling like a dinosaur.
>
> C) Insist that you are now a "Sockasaurus Rex" and create an elaborate sock kingdom.

3. A child is crying because their banana broke in half. How do you respond?

> A) Calmly explain that the banana will taste the same either way.
>
> B) Empathize with their banana sadness and offer to find a whole one.
>
> C) Declare the banana has fainted from surprise and perform a dramatic banana rescue mission.

4. A child wants to tell you a very, very, very long story about a rock they found. You:

> A) Try to listen while tidying the room at the same time.
>
> B) Sit down, make eye contact, and let them tell the whole story in their own time.

C) Propose that the rock probably has a secret life and start co-inventing its wild backstory.

5. A child spills their cereal and gasps. You:

A) Quickly clean it up and remind them to be careful next time.

B) Assure them it's not a big problem, hand them a towel, and help clean up together.

C) Announce that the cereal just held a surprise escape mission and start chasing the fleeing Cheerios around the room.

Your Results:

Mostly A's: Efficiency Explorer!

You're focused on keeping things moving, keeping life on track. Beautiful! Just notice if you are leaving a little room for silliness, softness, and surprise. You can always pause for one more giggle. The train won't leave without you.

Mostly B's: Playful Companion!

You're tuned in, moving at the child's pace, and delighting in their world. Wonderful! You're offering your presence and your heart. Just peek at your practical tasks sometimes to keep your grown-up world humming along.

Mostly C's: Absurdity Adventurer!

You are fully in the Zone of pancake rescue squads, sock dinosaur parades, and cereal heist stories. Incredible! You're living the magic. Just remember to send that important email... sometime before bedtime.

Embracing Paradox

So... if we want to understand life deeply, we have to let a little absurdity in.
And that includes... paradox... two things that seem opposite can both be true.

Often, things are both: happy and sad, yes and no, simple and complex.
That's true inside us too.

You are powerful and powerless.
You are unique and just like everyone else.
You are the artist and the unfinished work.
You are the center of the universe and a speck of stardust.

Human beings are full of opposites and it can drive a linear mind crazy...
Just tell me what it is!
I don't know, it's both and more... and that's a precise answer.

The universe is a giant cosmic riddle that can't be solved with logic.
You can't fully analyze it; you have to feel it, live it, dance with it. Even scientists
discovered that reality is full of weird surprises:

Particles can be in two places at once.
Schrödinger's cat is both alive and dead at the same time.
It's not what we were taught to expect,
but it's how the universe actually works... in mysterious ways.

Paradox is where even the sharpest intellect lays down its tools
and steps into the mystery.
It means you're getting close to something real.
The universe, this world, your child, and you are far more mysterious and
magnificent than the mind can grasp.
This is a timeless truth, old as human reflection itself.

Over 2,500 years ago, Lao Tzu, the legendary sage behind the *Tao Te Ching*, offers this wisdom:

"True perfection seems imperfect.

Yet it is perfectly itself.

True fullness seems empty,

Yet it is fully present.

True straightness seems crooked.

True wisdom seems foolish.

True art seems artless."

Flow has its own intelligence... and in the Zone with a child,
we sometimes feel the hidden order within the seeming chaos.
We remember that the world isn't random after all,
it's just not easy to wrap our minds around it.

Flow is always orchestrating behind the scenes,
even when the mind gets puzzled.

Whether you're young or old, bold or quiet,
wherever you come from, whatever your story,
whoever you dream of becoming,
you are part of the great mystery.

You, too, are made of stardust and questions and light.
The universe took its time shaping you,
uniquely suited for your place in the great unfolding.

Closing Reflection Part Three

We have explored the Zone, traveled through the science of safety and the timelessness of the Forever Now. We have embraced the intelligence of absurdity and rediscovered the liberation that comes when we stop being the expert and start learning like a child again. There is a profound relief in this space.

Now that we are free from the pressure of needing all the answers, we are finally open to being surprised. Now that we understand how to be a safe harbor for our own nervous systems, we can truly be a safe harbor for others.

We have found our way into the Zone, and from this place, we are ready to look at a new-old way of walking through life together with children.

We are ready for Flow Companionship, where we walk this path together with children and our Inner Child.

Let's take a Doodle Break

Before we dive into the next Part, let's get into Doodle Flow. Take a moment to let yourself play. Let your non-dominant hand use your favorite pen and see what comes out first...spirals, circles or shapes that delight you, or something totally new? Perhaps even a not to yourself: *You're amazing!*

Enjoy your hand, the ink, and the Forever Now.

PART FOUR

In the Zone With Your Child

In this Part, we'll explore what it means to step beyond the role
of parent, caregiver, or teacher and also be a companion in the Zone.

Now, you're not the one with all the answers.
You're the one who stays curious.
Who slows down long enough to notice the sparkle in a child's eye when
they're figuring something out.
Who plays, not to entertain, but to join the wonder.

To be a Flow Companion is to move from control to connection.
Learning becomes a dance. Emotions become doorways.
And play becomes a shared language.

You'll be inspired to share the beauty and inspiration you find in life
and open yourself to the wonders your child will show you in return.

You'll see how trust becomes the ground beneath everything.
This is where relationship becomes the real curriculum.
And love becomes the method.
Let's begin.

10

INVITATION 10

Being a
Flow Companion

Welcome, dear grown-up, to the best job you never applied for:
companion to a tiny magical human.

In a world that often feels too fast, too loud, or too uncertain,
a grown-up who has time is something extraordinary.

Not an expert. Not a fixer.
But a loving presence. A soft landing place.
A companion. A sidekick. A mapmaker of joy.

This is where you're not only the adult
and you start becoming also a co-adventurer.

Whether you're a parent, grandparent, auntie, uncle, teacher, friend, or

any loving grown-up woven into a child's life... the child in your care, your

classroom, your life, or your heart, is also a bit *your child* for the time being.
This is not about ownership, but about relationship.

Your presence is the magic that helps a child's world unfold.
This kind of magic has shaped childhoods, and sometimes, the whole world.

How Flow Companionship Shapes the World

The connection between a child and a caring grown-up has always been a force for transformation. Let's go on a journey of Flow Companionship through history:

Mrs. Wright, Frank Lloyd Wright's Mother placed beautiful architectural prints above her baby's crib and gave him building blocks before he could speak. She told him he would be a great architect, and he believed her. She saw his inner world before he had the words for it. Her early belief fed the Zone of a boy who would one day design buildings that feel alive.

Albert Einstein's Papa Hermann comforted his six-year-old son while he was sick in bed and gave him a gift: a small compass. That magnetic needle captivated little Albert and stirred something deep: What invisible forces guide the world? His father didn't know it then, but that single act of companionship sparked the theory of relativity.

Anne Sullivan, Helen Keller's Companion and Teacher entered the scene when Helen was wild with frustration, unable to speak, see, or hear. Anne, just twenty years old and half-blind herself, used patience, creativity, and relentless love to make a bridge. She spelled "W-A-T-E-R" into Helen's palm as water poured over it. Suddenly, meaning broke through. Anne didn't just teach Helen language; she opened the world to her.

Mr. Cousteau, Jacques's Father gifted his curious son with books, tools, and time. While Jacques splashed in a backyard pool with homemade goggles, his father supported his wonder. That early flow, unhurried and encouraged, became a lifelong devotion. One day, Jacques Cousteau would dive into the deep blue and reveal the ocean's mysteries to humanity.

Mrs. Bertha Flowers, Maya Angelou's Mentor offered love through silence. As young Maya chose not to speak for nearly five years, Bertha kept handing her poetry and presence. She never pushed. She stayed. And when Maya Angelou's voice returned, it carried the weight of truth, beauty, and the fire to free others.

Miss Mazzy, Nina Simone's Piano Teacher sat with little Eunice Waymon when she was only three, watching her play hymns by ear on the family piano. Miss Mazzy, a white woman in segregated North Carolina, paid for her lessons when no one else would. She nurtured a dream many would have dismissed. And through her presence, she helped birth the voice of Nina Simone, whose music later roared through concert halls, protest marches, and hearts worldwide.

Eustacia Cutler, Temple Grandin's Mother refused every limiting prognosis. When doctors said her daughter would never talk, she said, "Watch her." She found creative therapies and poured love into the cracks. Her presence gave Temple room to think in pictures and develop revolutionary insights.

Cynthia Bradley, Misty Copeland's Ballet Teacher watched as a thirteen-year-old girl stepped into ballet class for the first time, and danced en pointe within months. Cynthia saw what others overlooked: a gifted dancer with untapped potential. She brought Misty into her home, gave her space to grow, and protected her delicate zone of focus. Because of that sheltering presence, Misty became the first Black female principal dancer with the American Ballet Theatre.

Ziauddin Yousafzai, Malala's Father ran a small school in Pakistan and refused to clip his daughter's wings. When others said girls should stay silent, he said, "Speak, daughter. The world must hear you." He treated her not as a future wife, but a future world-changer. That trust was the foundation beneath Malala's courage to speak up for girls' education at the United Nations.

A Flow Companion may feel like they're doing nothing special. But in a child's inner world, it might be everything.

Children Are Not Little Adults

To truly attune to a child, we must understand something essential… Children are not miniature versions of adults. Their entire being is still forming: their nervous system, cognition, emotional regulation, and sense of self. This is something many adults forget or never truly understood. Children aren't intentionally bad, selfish, or manipulative. They simply can't be. They're doing the best they can with the tools they have: tiny bodies, tender hearts, and developing brains.

They don't process language and logic the way most adults do. What they do is mirror us, especially our emotional tone, our energy, and our unconscious patterns. They reflect both what we mean to model and what we don't realize we're showing. This is how they survive. And in a way, it's a genius design: their mirroring invites us to grow the very compassion they need to grow their own.

This is also why traditional discipline often doesn't teach children what we hope it will. Scolding, yelling, isolating, threatening, or giving the silent treatment rarely reaches the heart of what a child needs to learn. It overwhelms their nervous system, leaving them feeling rejected, abandoned, or even unsafe.

To us, it may look like a lesson. To them, it feels like loss. And the younger the child, the more these reactions backfire. Young children are neurologically incapable of learning complex social concepts, like self-discipline or respectful boundaries, through words alone. They learn through presence, modeling, and connection.

What they need most is a steady adult nervous system, not more rules or consequences.

They are always asking, "Am I safe? Am I loved? Am I welcome as I am?"
And when the answer is yes, learning and growth naturally follow.

And the same was true for you when you were little. You, too, were doing your best with a growing brain and a sensitive nervous system, trying to feel safe in a world that didn't always understand what you needed. If you were met with punishment, withdrawal, or emotional disconnection instead of warm guidance, you likely adapted the only way you could...by hiding parts of yourself, disconnecting, or trying harder to please.

And here's the tender truth: your inner child is still learning this way. Even now, as an adult, when someone gives you the silent treatment, yells at you, rejects you, or tries to "teach you a lesson" through disconnection or control, it can reawaken that same ancient ache. That small part of you doesn't feel corrected, it feels abandoned. And that wound doesn't vanish with age. Because no matter how old we are, we do not grow through shame. We grow through love, through being seen, through gentle presence and compassionate boundaries that help us feel safe enough to stay connected.

This is why healing isn't just about understanding what happened; it's about re-learning how to treat ourselves and each other in ways that truly work.

And ultimately, this is a path each of us must walk for ourselves. You are the only one who can reparent your Inner Child with the consistency, patience, and love that was once missing. But the beautiful thing is, you can. You can become the presence you always needed.

And as you become a Flow Companion for the children in your life, something miraculous happens: the two paths of healing begin to nourish one another.

For many of us, it is easier to offer kindness to a child than it is to offer it to ourselves. But as you practice meeting a child's "mess" with grace and their "loudness" with a steady heart, you are secretly practicing that same mercy for your own younger self.

Every time you tell a child, "You are safe, you are loved, and you are welcome exactly as you are," your own Inner Child hears it, too.

The Art of Companionship

Flow companionship is where friendship and guidance meet. The word companion comes from the Latin *com panis*. It means "the one with whom you share bread." It's such a simple, beautiful image: sitting together, breaking bread, not from a place of superiority, but from the side. Shoulder to shoulder. Eye to eye.

Companionship begins when we drop roles and hierarchies. It's not about who knows more. It's about *being with*.

You still offer care and protection, but you're also invited to relax and enter the child's world with warmth and curiosity. You're present without pressure.

A flow companion is more than a role; it's a way of being.
It's saying, "I'll walk with you. I'll learn with you.
I'll see you as you are, and I'll let you see me too."

You get to be real. To make mistakes. But you stay rooted in love. You tend to the bond with patience, playful connection, and gentle repair when needed.

And above all, you realize: children are never against you. They're simply trying to stay true to themselves.

You Can Be Both: Guide and Friend

We often hear that you can't be "friends" with your child. That friendship implies a loss of authority, or that being on an equal level with a child undermines the necessary power dynamic of adult–child relationships.
But that's not the whole story.

We can absolutely form a respectful friendship with children, one where we are the steady, reliable guide, and they trust our leadership because we've earned it. Just like you can be friends with a mountain guide, a mentor, or a wise elder, you can be in a relationship where you laugh together, share openly, and still know who's holding the map when it counts.

Friendship doesn't erase roles. It brings humanity to them.

In a friendship of mutual respect, children feel safe to tell the truth. They don't obey out of fear; they listen because they've experienced that our guidance is trustworthy and good for them. The tone we set...warm, steady, playful, or firm when needed, is what teaches them how to respond. They learn that kindness and respect can coexist with leadership. And so, they grow into people who lead that way too.

This kind of relationship becomes even more important as children grow into teenagers. If we haven't established real connection, they'll seek advice, understanding, and belonging elsewhere. And in a world swirling with confusing messages, online personas, and social media pressures, that "elsewhere" can lead them into all kinds of heartache and disorientation.

Teenagers are hungry for someone who sees them without judgment. Someone steady enough to handle their confusion, bold enough to hold boundaries, and loving enough to help them find themselves in the maze. When we show up as that companion who is willing to listen and to stay close even when things get messy, we become a lighthouse in their storm. Sometimes the only one.

Of course, this kind of relationship isn't always easy. And it doesn't mean being permissive or never saying no. But there's an undercurrent that holds it all together: a current of connection that deepens over time.

In every thriving adult–child relationship I've seen, whether in families or classrooms, there's a moment where the roles soften and two humans meet. In shared laughter. In grief. In creative play. In that flicker of "We're in this together."

In these moments you see the world through their eyes... and you let it change you.

That's friendship and companionship. And it keeps your bond alive.

A Soft Landing Place

Many of us grew up inside harshness. Not always in loud voices, but in the air around us... in schools that praised compliance over curiosity, homes shaped by survival, jobs that rewarded numbing out. We were taught to brace. To toughen up.

But a child... sensitive, sensing, open... is not meant to grow in a storm of stress. Harshness shuts down the pathways that allow us to connect, learn, and thrive.

That's where you come in. You can be a sanctuary. Not another adult giving orders with a kind voice, but a steady, kind-hearted ally who sees the child as wonderful, just as they are.

Sometimes children fall apart in front of the safest person in the room. Maybe that's you. And you wonder, *Why me?* But it's because you're doing it right. Their meltdown is a sign of trust. Their nervous system says, "Here I can exhale."

The most loving response is to offer a soft blanket, or making hot chocolate without comment. Or just being still, so the child's heart knows they are not alone. These small gestures say:

"You don't have to talk. You don't have to please me.
I'm right here, and you're safe with me."

That kind of presence can be more healing than any good advice.

Don't Lose Heart

If your child is exposed to a lot of stress, whether it's school pressure, social challenges, or the strain of trying to meet someone else's expectations, please don't lose heart. When a child has even one person who welcomes their questions, follows their fascinations, and mirrors their worth, self-trust begins to grow. They learn it's safe to explore, to feel, to take risks, because someone truly believes in them.

Pain will still come. That's life. But alongside it, they'll carry a memory... the memory of learning through joy and safety. That memory becomes an inner companion and a felt sense of "I can meet the world with curiosity, not just defensiveness."

You can't protect a child from every storm. But you can show them what it feels like to be warm and safe somewhere in the world, even just for a little while.
And that little may change their inner landscape for good.

You're the Keeper of the Flame

Every child arrives with a spark.
You see it in the way they laugh at the smallest things, the way they disappear into play, the way their eyes light up when something fascinates them. Curiosity, imagination, courage, and wonder shine brightly in them from the very beginning.

But the world can be noisy and hurried. Expectations grow. Schedules fill the days. Little by little, that flame can flicker under the winds of pressure, comparison, and self-doubt.
This is where you come in.
You are the keeper of the flame.
You protect the conditions in which their spark can keep glowing. By offering presence instead of pressure. By allowing curiosity instead of constant correction. By seeing the unique light in this child and trusting it enough to let it grow.

Sometimes keeping the flame alive is simple:
watching together, listening closely, laughing at something silly, or giving a child the time to follow their own fascination.

And something extraordinary happens in those moments.
The child's flame grows stronger.
And yours begins to glow again too.
Because the spark children carry is not only theirs.
It belongs to all of us.

It is the same living fire that once burned so brightly in our own childhood.

When you protect that spark in a child, you are not only shaping their future.
You are healing something across generations.
And that flame once protected, can light many others.

~ *Did You Ever Have a Flow Companion Moment?*~

Think back to your own childhood. Was there someone, a big-hearted adult, who took the time to tell you a story, to explain something patiently, Someone who showed you how to make amends, or helped you discover something you still love today?

And now, think of a moment when a child showed you something important to them, maybe a drawing, a Lego creation, or a new skill, and you paused, listened, and really enjoyed being part of it.

Those moments, whether received or given, leave a lasting imprint of love.

Everyone Can Be a Flow Companion

Whether you're a parent, teacher, caregiver, a child development expert or simply someone who loves children, flow companionship is for you.

Even though many ideas in this book are inspired by Maria Montessori and other brilliant educators, you don't need a degree to do this. Parenting classes and educational methods can be wonderful supports, but they're not the heart of the work. At the heart of it, is your relationship with the child in front of you. In fact, sometimes those very trainings, well-meaning as they may be, can become a layer between you and the child. They fill your head with scripts and strategies, and suddenly you're thinking,

"What am I supposed to do in this situation?" instead of asking,
"What does this child need right now?"

Presence and kindness can't be replaced by method. Only an open heart can see what's true in the moment. What you really need is your willingness to slow down and truly see a child. The will to stay safe, even when you're upset. Sometimes, the courage to get a little weird. The trust to let curiosity lead and the heart follow.

I learned this from my mentors, Rebeca and Mauricio Wild, who inspired a global movement of experimental schools rooted in Flow Learning. They once ordered a full set of Montessori materials from the Netherlands to their home in Ecuador, eager to support their young son's learning. But when the boxes arrived, their son didn't touch the elegant learning tools. He was mesmerized by the packaging, the cardboard, the crumpled paper, and the space inside the box. He played for hours.

And Rebeca didn't correct him. She watched. She followed. She gave him more boxes. Because he was already learning, deeply, joyfully, on his own terms. I never forgot that.

And I never forgot this story about Maria Montessori. Before she developed her method, she was a physician working in a hospital. There, she saw something astonishing: the children, confined to sterile beds, began gathering breadcrumbs. Not to eat, but to play. They arranged them in patterns, named them, built tiny worlds. And she didn't stop them. She saw something sacred: The impulse to learn is already inside the child.

Her great experiment became this: to prepare environments where that impulse could thrive. That was her most profound contribution. Not the tools. Not the method. But the trust.

This is what brought me here too... watching closely, listening deeply, learning from the quiet clues children offer.

And you can do that too...in your home, in your classroom, on the playground. Just like over a hundred years ago, you may find children building with breadcrumbs and cardboard and crumpled paper.

Times may change, but the message remains:
Children show us what matters.
All we have to do is slow down enough to notice.

A Special Note for Chosen Family

Not everyone raising a child is a parent. And not everyone who nurtures a child lives in the same home, shares their DNA, or holds a legal role. And this truth is woven into many of the world's oldest and most beautiful traditions.

In West African culture, and carried forward through the African diaspora, there is a saying: it takes a village to raise a child. In Black American communities, close family friends are often called *Auntie* or *Uncle*, not as a formality, but as a genuine claim of belonging.

In Latino families, the tradition of *compadrazgo* means that godparents, *padrinos* and *madrinas*, are true co-raisers of a child, bound by love and responsibility.

In many Caribbean households, that same spirit flows through generations, where neighbors, elders, and chosen family all hold a piece of a child's upbringing.

Among Indigenous communities across the Americas, elders and extended family have always shared the sacred work of guiding the young.
In Hawaiian culture, *ohana* reminds us that family is not defined by blood alone.

Or, maybe you're the neighbor who waves and smiles. Maybe you're the teacher who listens without rushing. Maybe you're the godparent who sends postcards. Maybe you're just someone who notices when a child is struggling and chooses to see them clearly.

You don't have to "have kids" to have a role. You can still be a Flow Companion, a steady presence, a soft place to land, and a spark of joy. One smile and one moment of genuine attention can stay with a child for life.

And if you're reading this book without children of your own: thank you. You may be more important than you know.

A Welcome to Our Elders

In many families, the circle of care includes people who have already lived a long and rich life, elders of every kind, two or three generations deep. Whether you are a daily presence or an occasional visitor, your role is far from small.

You bring something no one else can. Stories that only you carry. A rhythm that comes from having lived. Warmth that children feel before they can even name it. Your presence alone can be a source of deep comfort and joy.

You have seen the world change, weathered seasons, raised children, and held a life full of meaning. And now you find yourself part of a new chapter, one where your love and experience are genuinely needed.

Sometimes that role feels clear. Sometimes it feels uncertain, especially when the childhoods unfolding around you look so different from the ones you remember. Parenting has changed. Childhood has changed. And it can be disorienting, even for the most loving and generous of hearts.

But here is what hasn't changed: children still need to feel seen. They still need to feel safe. They still need to know that someone delights in them. And you already know how to do that.

You don't have to parent again. You get to be something else, something just as precious. A witness. A storyteller. A Flow Companion. Someone who sits beside a child and makes them feel that this moment, right now, is enough.

You can join a child's world through listening, sharing stories, making art, playing games, gardening, taking silly walks, or simply sitting together in the quiet. You can follow their curiosity and add to their inspiration.

To the parents and caregivers reading this: invite your elders in, and before they arrive, or in a quiet moment together, have a real conversation. Not a list of rules, but a sharing of hearts.

Tell them what your days look like. Tell them what matters most to you in your home, the rhythms you are trying to protect, the values you are trying to live. Not because you expect them to do it perfectly, but because when they understand the why behind your choices, they are far more likely to feel like partners rather than guests who are tiptoeing around invisible lines.

And to the elders themselves: your love still speaks fluently. Children hear it, even when no words are spoken. This new (old) way of learning in flow, it was made for you too. There is big, beautiful room for you in it.

11

INVITATION 11
We Pull Each Other Into Presence

Presence is something we share with children, and they share with us. Every real connection is a two-way invitation: sometimes a child pulls us out of our heads and into the moment; sometimes we offer them the steady ground of our own attention. It's a dance, an exchange. It's being alive together.

Neuroscience shows that when two people are truly present with each other, their bodies and brains begin to sync. Heartbeats slow down. Stress levels drop. Brain waves attune. This is co-regulation, and it's how humans have always found safety, comfort, and courage. And we co-regulate not only emotions, but also attention, curiosity, and presence.

Children are wired to seek this kind of resonance. When they play, they're inviting us to join their world, a world where time disappears, and every pebble can be a doorway to wonder. When we step in with curiosity, we let ourselves be changed. Their joy becomes contagious and their presence wakes up our own.

And the invitation flows both ways. As children pull us into the Forever Now, we open doors for them: art, music, stories, rituals that will live in them long after they've grown. Every moment we truly meet a child, we remind one another how good it is to be here, together, in the Forever Now. And before you realize it, you've crossed the threshold together, into that current of doing, being, and becoming.

Joining a Child in Their Zone

Children pull us out of our thoughts and into the moment simply because they are so fully in theirs. It feels like they hand us a permission slip:

Come here. Let this be enough.
Let this be interesting. Let's be here together.

At first, you simply watch. A child drawing endless spirals.
Arranging building blocks. Comforting their doll.
Explaining a game they invented.
Sharing a world only they can see.

You may need to hold yourself back from teaching or correcting.
Just notice. Just breathe beside them. It may feel like rest.

And sometimes an impulse rises: *Maybe I could draw too…*
What if I made something just because it delights me?

When you join a child in play, you enter their world.
Let them take the lead.
Notice what delights them.
Go along for the ride and witness a budding personality being comfortable and busy in a world of their own making.

There are many playful and embodied ways to enter the Zone with a child, through movement, games, shared laughter, and physical play. In my earlier book *Flow to Learn*, I explore these pathways in depth. Here, rather than listing specific activities, we turn to the deeper conditions that make these moments of connection possible.

Sharing What You Love

One of the most magical parts of Flow Companionship is when a child wants to know more about something you love. Your child might be captivated by the simplest things you do: chopping vegetables with care or fixing a bike with focus. In those moments, we show children what it means to love the process, while engaged in something real.

Or you might offer a simple invitation, such as a walk with no agenda, a beautiful picture book to explore, or tinkering with a few art supplies. These small invitations build trust, ease, and belonging.

Let Curiosity Lead, No Strings Attached

If you invite your child and they don't want to join your activity, don't take it personally. Every child is on their own path, moving through the world with their own rhythm, needs, and curiosities. Your invitation is simply that: an open door, not a test.

When a child says "no thanks," it isn't a rejection of you, it's just a moment where their attention is pulled somewhere else. And that's perfectly okay.

Some days you might share a project. Other days, togetherness happens side by side, as each of you does your own thing in flow side by side.

Sometimes the best way to spark shared joy isn't through direct invitation, but by creating inspiration in the environment.

Set out a tray with beads and strings, or place a looking glass within easy reach. Maybe you let them explore your jewelry, help you "inspect" the car, or discover something new in the kitchen. These open-ended invitations let a child's curiosity come out to play, no pressure attached.

Enjoying Music Together

Music is one of the most direct gateways to the Zone, for both adults and children. When we truly surrender to it, music carries us.

Studies show that music can influence neural oscillations, entraining our brainwaves to match the rhythm, tone, and tempo of what we're hearing.
In simpler terms: our nervous systems start dancing with the music.

And when you listen with your child your nervous systems can harmonize with each other, too.

This is why shared music moments can feel so good...
whether you're listening to peaceful piano, dancing to a fun tune,
harmonizing your voices, or making music as a family ensemble.

It's co-regulation through vibration.
A reset button for body and mind.

For a child, whose nervous system is shaped moment by moment by their environment, music can become a powerful tool of self-regulation, expression, and connection, especially when shared with someone they love.

Create your signature playlist: Find the songs that move both of you. These will become your shared melodies of the Forever Now. So next time you're not sure how to reconnect, start with a song.

Finding Beauty Together

Beauty is another invitation into presence that needs no words. Something that captures our attention with reverence, slows us down, and opens the heart.

Don't let someone else define beauty for you or your child.
Find your own lens. Make it wide. Make it loving.
Because the more beauty you see, the more beautiful life becomes.

Step out into the world and find beauty together. For your child, maybe it's a shiny red firetruck, a glitter sticker, or a swirl of colors in a painting. It might be whimsical, simple, or bright. Maybe you share their love for flowers, bugs, or crystals.

What matters is that you look together. Discover together.
Let their sense of wonder meet your appreciation, and let beauty be a bridge.

Visit art galleries, museums, or sculpture parks. Watch dance, poetry, and theater. Admire craftsmanship such as handmade pottery, careful embroidery, and study the lines of great architecture.

Your child may not understand or value the same beauty you do in that moment, but it stays with them. These impressions are stored in their memory, like seeds. Later in life, they may walk into a room or a landscape, and something will stir. A feeling will rise. That early sense of beauty will surface, and feel like home.

Children need companions who say, "Look. Listen. Feel this."

When we show children many kinds of beauty, we're giving them a way of seeing that nourishes and sustains.

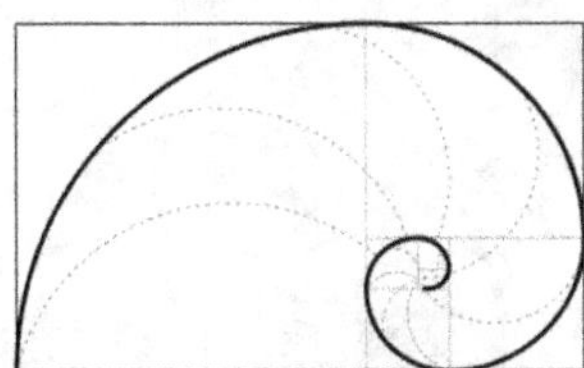

Sharing Time in Nature

Our Original Flow Teacher

If you've ever watched a child in nature, you've seen it: you don't need to tell them what to do. Something inside them wakes up... a sense of inner guidance, curiosity, and freedom. Before you know it, they find sticks, arrange rocks into patterns, or squat to study a beetle.

Nature beckons children and grown-ups into presence, engagement, and wonder. It doesn't need instructions, and it doesn't judge. It simply offers raw materials: sticks, mud, leaves, light, water, gravity. And children respond with joy, focus, and a deep sense of rightness.

Toddlers follow this instinct instantly. And even older children, those who have begun to worry about what others think, can find themselves again in the wild.

Give them time and maybe some encouragement, and you'll see it happen. A branch becomes a sword or a staff. A tree becomes a lookout post or a friend. A stream becomes an engineering challenge, or a place to feel weightless again.

When a child finds a special rock, or a hidden nook between roots, or when they lie belly-down to peer at a worm, they are not just playing... they are reconnecting. They are in dialogue with the living world.
And in that dialogue, they come home to themselves.

As a Flow Companion you can simply be there with them, offer a safe anchor, snacks and water, enjoy the scenery, and let it happen.

Learning Something New Together

There's a rare magic that unfolds when grown-up and child stand together at the edge of the unknown: both beginners, both a bit clumsy. Whether you're trying to juggle oranges, learn the first chords on a ukulele, or stumble through the pronunciation of a new language, something precious happens: the playing field becomes level, and you can say, "I don't know... let's find out together."

You don't need to have all the answers, it's actually more encouraging for your child when they see that you are learning, too.

You might notice your child taking the lead, inventing new approaches, or boldly embracing failure as part of the game. You might find yourself cheering each other on, celebrating first tries and tiny victories that feel monumental. Suddenly, mistakes become part of the fun, and the process becomes richer than any polished outcome.

In these moments, you're sending a message that says,
"It's safe to try, it's okay to stumble, and we're in this together."

This is the heart of Flow Companionship: meeting your child on the fresh ground of not knowing, and letting discovery be the real destination.

So, let the kitchen be a science lab, the living room a dance studio, the backyard a wild expedition. Let curiosity lead, and watch how your connection deepens, as you're both open to what's possible.

In the end, you'll have gained more than a new skill,
you'll have built trust, memories, and a shared language of courage.

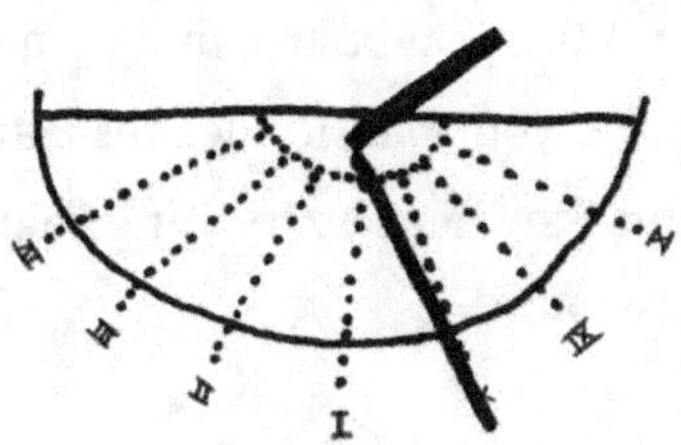

A Note on the Side:
Rolling My Eyes Yet Learning Everything

Some children will leap into a project you're offering. Others, like me as a child, might meet it with a sigh and a shrug. I habitually rolled my eyes at everything my Mom offered. She was a wonderful Flow Companion, always crafting, baking, collecting, and pointing out the beauty around us. But I lived in a state of low-key resistance with her. Maybe for reasons I didn't understand back then. Maybe because I just needed to feel separate. Who knows?

But wow… am I glad she did it anyway.

Every year, she made seasonal ornaments, she baked cookies, and collected pinecones and flowers. On our walks, she'd tell me the names of trees and wildflowers, lighting up when she saw something rare, "Look, look! The first crocus of spring!"

And me… I'd say, "Yeah, yeah, Mom."

But underneath the shrug, I was so happy she was doing it.

I loved that it was happening, even if I couldn't show it.

She let me come close, drift away, join in for a little or not at all. Sometimes I just watched her with one eye while pretending not to care. But I remember every flower she named, every cozy moment, and every tradition. Her joy etched the memories into me.

What I realize now is that she did it for herself, too.

She didn't need me to be enthusiastic for it to matter.

She gave me the freedom to join when I was ready,

and that made all the difference.

So take heart, if your child isn't fully on board, find something you love and do it anyway. Your joy has impact and your passion leaves traces. They may not show it now, but they're watching, and they hear everything that's going on around them. And in your presence, they are learning.

The Deeper Magic

Being in the Zone with children, may look simple from the outside...

But something deeper is happening.

A very primal need can be fulfilled for both of you:

The need to be held by presence.

For children this is powerful.

When this need is met, some behavioral challenges may naturally dissolve.

What looked like defiance may have been a call for connection.

What looked like resistance may have been a longing to be felt.

When connection lands, the system settles.

The whole day can shift.

And so often, magic happens for the grown-ups too.

Let's say you've been searching for a job, scrolling online,

trying to make things happen but your mind is tight, your energy scrambled.

But when you're able to peel yourself away and give your child ten minutes of

real presence, you create a different internal state,

and that inner shift begins to ripple outward.

When you return to your search, something has shifted.

Perhaps you notice an opportunity you missed.

Perhaps you even find an invitation waiting in your inbox.

This is not a guarantee or a formula.

It's an invitation to experiment.

When we drop the worry and urgency, we often see more clearly how supported

we actually are. We move from reaction to co-creation.

The doors you open when you slow down may lead to places you never could

have pushed your way into.

And then things really can rearrange. Maybe not instantly, but subtly and steadily.

This is what happens when presence becomes the anchor.

And this comes from lived, anecdotal experience: life often seems especially generous when children are involved.

Held by Boundaries and Free to Connect

As you've allowed yourself to be pulled into presence, and joined your child's world, and as you shared what you love, and explored the Forever Now together, you've already started to feel the foundation of the deeper layer of your relationship: being rooted within your boundaries.

When a child knows they are safely held by the loving boundaries between you, they begin to trust not just you, but themselves, and life.

That's where we go next.

12

INVITATION 12
Rooted in Boundaries

Saying no is one of the most challenging acts of love. We want to say yes, because we care, because we wish we could make life easier. And because saying no often means facing the intensity of a child's feelings. It means withstanding their heartbreak, their tears, their protests, and still staying rooted.

This is why it helps to pause and zoom all the way out to gain a higher perspective and remember why boundaries matter so much in the first place.

When we step back, we see that boundaries are not obstacles to connection, but the framework that allows it to flourish.

When you stand in the truth of your boundaries,
you free not just yourself, but your child.

You teach that your voice matters, and so does theirs.
That love can hold disagreement.
That worth is not tied to compliance.

You show them that boundaries and connection are not opposites;
they walk hand in hand.

Where I End and You Begin

Why do flowers bloom in a certain number of petals?
Why does music require silence to become melody?

Boundaries are part of the great design of life.

Everything that lives has a shape.

Everything that flows is held by form.

From the spiral of a snail shell to the orbit of planets,

life unfolds within limits.

We often think of boundaries as something negative,

a no that hurts. But the deepest kind of boundary isn't harsh.

It's sacred.

In nature, all beauty follows pattern.

And every pattern is born of a limit:

the edge between this and that,

between sound and silence,

between thing and no-thing.

A sacred boundary isn't a no out of fear.

It's a yes to the shape of your soul.

It's about the relief that comes from knowing,

"This is me. This is you. This is ours."

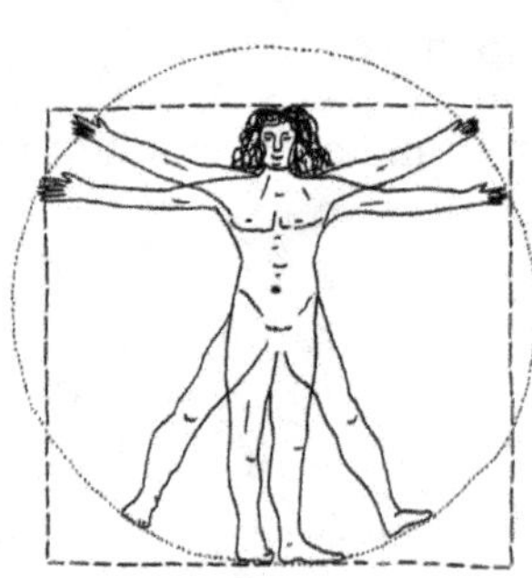

This Is Me, This Is You, This Is Ours

This is a sacred boundary between adult and child.

I am the adult.

You are the child.

Each of us whole. Each of us real.

This is me. This is you.

And this space between us is ours.

Like two circles overlapping, we meet in the middle.

Sometimes our lives overlap a lot.

When you are young, I carry more. I hold you close.

I help you feel safe in the world.

My rhythm helps you find your own.

And as you grow, the space between us shifts.

You become more you. I stay rooted in me.

And still, we belong to each other.

Not in ownership, but in love.

You are not mine to shape like clay.

You are not here to make me feel loved, or calm, or worthy.

You are here to become who you are.

And I am here to become who I am, too.

I say no, not to reject you, but to protect what matters.

I say no, not to control you, but to honor the shape of life.

You can lean on me, but I won't lose myself in you.

You can be angry with me, and I will still love you.

I can say no to you, and still hold you with tenderness.

Because love is not the same as giving in.

And boundaries are not the end of closeness,
they are the beginning of trust.

This is me. This is you.
And this is love that can last.

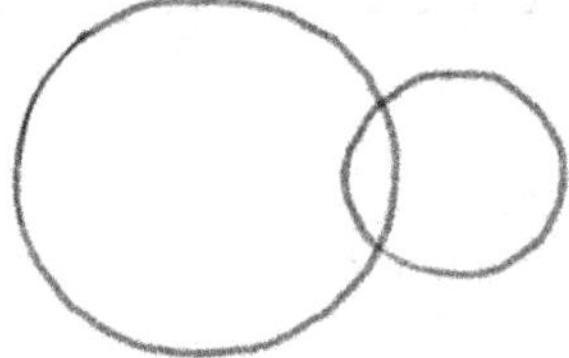

The Relief of Letting Go

There is a deep peace that arrives when we realize we do not have to carry what isn't ours. So often, without even noticing, we take on a child's world as if it were our responsibility to fix, to smooth, or to lift. We imagine that their frustration reflects our shortcomings, or that their triumph somehow belongs to us.

But in the Zone, another truth reveals itself.
Both the struggle and the sparkle belong to the child.

When a child grapples with a difficult task, it is their holy struggle.
When they light up with a breakthrough, it is their moment to shine.

And of course, we share it with them. We laugh with them, we celebrate with them, and we feel the ache of their sadness when life is heavy.

But we do this as companions and stewards, not as the owners of their experience. You stand beside them, not in place of them.

And when the moment passes, you return to yourself, centered and whole, so they can return to themselves too.

It is a profound relief to realize you don't have to manage a child's emotions or manufacture their joy. You only have to be the steady, loving presence that holds the space where it all happens.

Stewardship
and the Boundaries of Love

Children are not born into an empty world. They were born into a story already in motion… a home with rhythms, a culture with spoken and unspoken expectations, a place where things work in a certain way.

As magical and sovereign as children are, they can't possibly understand all
of that on their own.

Many things need to be taught. Not once, not as a scolding, but kindly and consistently, over time. When we step back too far and say, "Let them figure it out," without offering guidance or context, it doesn't lead to empowerment. It often leads to confusion, insecurity, and behavior that gets misread as "defiance," but is really just a child looking for the frame.

That's where we grown-ups come in. We are the bridge.
We show with kindness: "Look, here's how we do this."
"Look, here's what's okay in our home / classroom, and what's not."

This is loving orientation.
The act of helping a child feel safe enough to thrive.

A child who knows where the limits are, who's been taught, lovingly,
where structure holds them, is more free, not less.
In clarity, they can relax.
They can explore. They can play, create, and even push back,
because they know someone is walking beside them, holding the frame steady.

And when you teach these things with warmth and patience,
something beautiful happens: children feel proud.
Because someone cared enough to help them grow
into someone others love being around.

Respect Is a Two-Way Bridge

Love and freedom thrive within the frame of mutual respect. Respect doesn't mean blind obedience. It means honoring each other's space, dignity, and humanity. We teach it first and foremost by modeling it: listening deeply, speaking kindly, and treating even a child's no with care.

There are moments when modeling isn't enough. When a child yells at you, hits you, or speaks in a way that dishonors the relationship.
And in those moments, it's okay, even it's essential, to say:
"No. This stops now."
Every adult who spends time with children knows that moment.
It's power and truth rising up when disrespect crosses a line. It's when a clean, decisive boundary is needed that stops the behavior without shaming the child.

Many children actually need to feel this energy sometimes, because they are testing boundaries to find out where they are. It's how they feel safe.
It's how they learn, "Oh… this person is the leader. I can relax."

It's a gift to teach children that their anger and disappointment are welcome, but cruelty is not. They are still loved, even when they're upset, but they are not allowed to hurt you or another. This doesn't squash the child's spirit; it gives them scaffolding to grow into someone who can love fiercely and respect deeply.

"You don't have to agree with me, but I won't let you speak to me like that. Here's how you can say that, so I will listen."

This is a moment of clarity that teaches how to be in connection without harming others. And we say it not with shame or threat, but with clarity and firmness.

Respect is not fear. It's not blind obedience.
Respect is a sacred way of saying:
"I see you. And I ask you to see me too."

A Child's Boundaries

Boundaries aren't just something we do to children; they are something we live together with them, every day, as they grow. In every adult-child relationship, there comes a moment when the child's no emerges.

Let's feel into a child's first no... why it arises, what it reveals, and how honoring this moment shapes our connection to them for life.

A Child's Sacred No

In the beginning, there is no separation.
Your child is a part of you. Not metaphorically, but literally.
They lived inside your body... or in your arms, on your chest,
cradled in your lap.

Their heartbeat echoed in your own,
or in your ears as you held them close.
They needed you for everything.

Of course you lived in union.
Of course you felt as one.

And for a while, you are.
You anticipate their needs, feel their pain,
read their breath like a second language.
You know them.

But then...something shifts.
A hand pushes away.
A spoon is thrown.
A little voice says, *no!*

And the arrow lands in the grown-up's heart.

Not because the child is wrong,

but because separation is hard.

Even when it's natural. Even when it's needed.

This *no* is not defiance.

It's individuation.

It's your child discovering where they end and you begin.

It's them learning, "I can be different from you... and still be loved."

And isn't that a lesson we're all learning...

parents, teachers, caregivers, coaches, guides...

You are not this child.

And you are still whole, even when they disobey or walk away.

Love does not dissolve in individuation. It deepens.

So yes... sometimes they'll break your rules,

your heart, your image of who they were supposed to be.

Sometimes they'll run off with the circus.

And still... you cherish them.

Not as an extension of yourself,

but as someone you are honored to witness.

This is the gift.

This is the grief.

This is the miracle.

Practicing Consent with Children

When we respect a child's "no," we give them more than a moment of power,
we give them a foundation for a life of respect.
They learn that their voice matters.
We show them that love does not require self-abandonment,
and that healthy relationships allow for both connection and difference.

This is how they grow into adults who know they can say "no" when something doesn't feel right, who don't confuse love with compliance, or kindness with erasing themselves for others.

In honoring your child's boundaries, you teach them to honor yours, too.

When we include children in decisions, especially those that affect their bodies or emotions, they'll *know* what's safe, and when things don't feel safe. This builds self-worth and teaches them to honor their own limits, as well as the boundaries of others. Consent lives in many layers:

Physical: You decide when and how you're touched.

Emotional: You don't have to absorb others' feelings to stay connected.

Mental: You choose which ideas and beliefs feel true for you.

That's where confidence begins.
And that's how we grow a world where
boundaries are beautiful,
and everyone feels safe to say yes or no.

Boundaries Open to Trust

Boundaries, lovingly held, do more than protect; they prepare the soil for trust.

Each time we honor a child's Sacred No, their nervous system receives a clear signal: "You are safe with me.
It's okay to be you. It's okay to have needs and preferences."

And as we all know, there are moments when we can't honor a child's no,
when life, safety, or responsibility asks something else of us.
The key is to honor a child's Sacred No *enough and when it truly matters,*
so that trust can grow.

In that safety, children open up to your guidance and to collaboration more willingly when it's truly needed. Your parenting and educational efforts begin to land in fertile soil.

Pause here and notice how your own body softens when both your boundary and your child's are respected. That settling feeling is the doorway to our next exploration.

13

INVITATION 13
Trust and Repair
Keys to Enduring Connection

If you want to earn a child's trust...real, lasting trust, learn to notice and meet their genuine needs. Every time a child's true need is honored, their trust in you grows a little more. Over time, these moments accumulate into an unshakeable foundation.

As you meet a child's genuine needs, you make everything else possible for them: empathy, play, learning, rest, repair, and joy. So what are these genuine needs? Let's look at the essentials.

Physical Needs

Softness and slowness. Nourishment and rest.

Freedom to move. Nurturing touch.

The felt sense: I am welcome here.

Emotional Needs

To feel without being too much.

To cry without being left.

To be mirrored with care, not fear.

Intellectual Needs

To ask why and be met with wonder.

To explore without punishment.

To think their own thoughts.

Spiritual Needs

A sense of connection and meaning.

To experience a world that feels alive and good.

(No spiritual explanations are required, though they can be beautiful.)

And just as important are your own genuine needs: Your need for rest, nourishment, presence, and meaning, they matter too. Flow Companionship is not about self-sacrifice. It's about co-regulation. When your needs are honored alongside your child's, trust deepens on both sides.

~ *A Day of Noticing* ~

Spend a day simply observing your child and yourself through the lens of genuine needs:

> ~ When does your child seem energized or drained?

> ~ What restores them: movement, stillness, touch, friends, play, solitude?

> ~ What do they reach for when no one tells them what to do?

Now ask yourself: What helps you come back to yourself?

End the day by writing one sentence:
"I saw their need for ___ today. And I saw my own need for ___."

When You Make a Wish Come True

and the Pathway of Possibility Lights Up

Beyond genuine needs, every child carries a wish in their heart.

Sometimes it's big and bold, a puppy, a treehouse, a trip to the ocean.

Sometimes it's quiet and tender... to be taken seriously, to be invited in.

Always, beneath the wish, there's something deeper:
the longing to be seen.

When we respond to that longing, we plant a seed that can transform a life.
Because when a child's true wish comes true, something happens in their whole being. Their body lights up. Their brain registers a new truth:
"It's safe to hope." and "The universe listens."

This is more than a sweet moment.
It's a neural pathway of self-worth being laid down.
It's a cellular memory of possibility that stays with them, long after the toy is forgotten or the day has passed. It reminds the child, later in life,
even in hard times:
"Good things are possible for me."

If a child's big wish, like a trip to Disneyland, a cat, or a pony isn't possible at the moment, you can create a vision board together, so you give that longing a place to land.

And when you can fulfill a wish, even a small one...
it becomes a firework moment.
An explosion of joy, of magic, of "yes!" in their body.
You showed a child that their longings are valuable,
their voice has power,
and that the world can sometimes... beautifully, unpredictably... say yes!

The Power of Your Loving Attention

Here's something radical but true: Children can feel seen in seconds.
When they enter your space, your home, classroom, or therapy room,
anywhere, and you pause, smile, look them in the eyes, and say,

"I'm so glad you're here." That might be the moment that saves them.

You can listen, even for just a moment. You can validate their questions,
their struggles, their wonderings.

You can say: "That makes sense." "I hear you." "You're not alone."

These are ways to help a child feel safe in the moment,
with you and with their activity.

Loving attention can happen in an instant, and it is the kind of presence any adult
can offer, a teacher, a family friend, a neighbor... a Flow Companion.

When a child feels your trust in them, they begin to trust in themselves.
This is the power of loving attention... to help a child feel safe and capable in
your presence.

The Art of Repair

One of the most important aspects of creating trust is repair after conflict.
Every relationship has moments of disconnection.
Sometimes it's a sharp word. A slammed door. A misunderstanding.
A moment where one or both of you pull away.

But the magic isn't in never getting it wrong. The magic is in coming back.
Whether you're seven or seventy, we all get overwhelmed.
We all miss the mark. And we all need to feel it's safe to return.

Real repair happens when both people, child and grown-up, or partner and friend,
feel the freedom to show up with honesty and tenderness, and without a fear of
punishment. And from that safety, repair can rise.

What Repair Is Not
Real repair is humble. It's brave.
It's about taking responsibility for impact, not defending intention.

In a world where apologies are often rushed, sugarcoated, or wrapped in ego,
it's important to model repair to children when we lose patience,
and be clear about what repair isn't.

Repair is not: "I'm sorry you feel that way." That's deflection.
It puts the emotion back on the other person
without acknowledging the action that caused it.

"Well, if you hadn't acted like that, I wouldn't have yelled." That's blame.
It teaches that someone else's behavior justifies unkindness.

"Fine. Sorry." That's reactivity.
It shuts the door on connection instead of opening it.

And repair is not pretending it didn't happen.
People remember the tone, the rupture, the moment the warmth disappeared.

When we pretend nothing happened, children learn to doubt themselves, or to bury pain.

What Repair Is

Real repair looks like pausing. Facing the moment honestly.
And saying something like: "I didn't like how I spoke earlier. I'm sorry.
Can we start over?"
"I got overwhelmed. That wasn't your fault. Let's try again, please?"
"I care about how that felt to you. I will do better next time."

Let Them See Repair Between Adults Too

Repair isn't just something we offer children.
It's something we practice in all our relationships.
And something children should witness.

When they see grown-ups say:
"Hey, I'm sorry I interrupted you earlier,"
or "I think I misunderstood, can we try again?" they learn that care, humility, and accountability are part of growing up, not something we outgrow.

They learn that kindness is strength.
That coming back to connection is a powerful skill.

If you're reading this and remembering moments you wish you'd handled differently, that's okay. That means your heart is awake.

Repair isn't a sign that something went wrong.
It's a sign that something matters.
That you care enough to mend the thread, to reach across the distance,
to say: "We're still us. We're okay."
And you both can grow inside the warmth between you.

A Wider Lens on Flow Companionship

The Mystery We're Meant to Honor

We are raising a generation unlike any before... sensitive, brilliant, evolving in mysterious ways. Even helpful models can't fully map what's unfolding for each child. As a Flow Companion you can release yourself from the pressure of having to fully understand a child in order to love and support them.

We don't need to understand the *why* to be present for the *who*.

The most powerful thing you can say is:
"I may not understand what this is for you. But I'm here for you."

And in the presence of that kindness, the child in front of you feels safe, your Inner Child exhales, and you remember how to breathe together again.

Tending Your Own Garden

To be this kind of unconditional love, you need also tend to your own garden.
You need a place to return to inside yourself.

A child doesn't need you to orbit them all the time.
What they need most is to know that you are available *when it matters*.

That you are not shaken by their aliveness; that you are your own center.
This is how trust grows.

Spoiler Alert: Love Lives Inside You

And here's something you might notice as you keep showing up as a companion in the Zone: the more love you give, the more love you feel.

It might not always come back from the same person,
or in the same moment, but it does come back.

The more you give love to your child, to yourself,
to the moment in front of you, the more love you see.

This whole world is a hide-and-seek game.
And love is the one doing the hiding.

It wears disguises: approval, attention, success,

the right clothes, the right words,

someone else finally saying "You're enough."

But one day, as you become more and more present to your own life,

you may feel a shift.

Not because everything got easier,

but because you became more grounded in what really matters to you.

You start to realize: Love is not a reward.

It's a frequency.

It's your superpower.

And no one can take it from you.

And when you live from that place of *already-loved*,

you give a child the most beautiful map of all:

Not one that leads them out into the world to go find love,

but one that leads them back home to themselves.

That's the kind of being with children that rewires the world.

Closing Reflection Part Four

Every moment you offer this kind of presence, anchored in your own enough-ness, you're not just shaping a child's world, you're rewriting your own story too. The care you extend outward returns to you, layer by layer, awakening the Inner Child who still longs for this same gentle attention.

So before you step into the next part, pause and notice:

How does it feel to know you can give, and receive, this quality of love?

How might your Inner Child want to be met, held, or invited into play right now?

As we turn the page, you'll discover that everything you wish to give a child is also medicine for your own heart.

The journey inward to meet your Inner Child is the next Invitation, because you, too, are worthy of all the presence, wonder, and unconditional love you so freely offer.

Space for Your Notes:

PART FIVE

In the Zone With Your Inner Child

This Part is devoted to the invisible one that's been with you the whole time: your Inner Child.

They've been riding along as you show up for children in classrooms, kitchens, parks, and epic snack negotiations.
And sometimes, just sometimes, they throw a little inner tantrum when no one's watching.

This is your invitation to turn inward and say to yourself:
"Hey… I see you Little One. You're coming with me now."

Because while you've been showing up for the children in front of you with love, patience, and snacks, you've also been healing something deep, wobbly, and holy inside yourself…

This is an invisible thread that's been running through the book.
Now it gets its moment to shine.

Let's invite your Inner Child into the circle…

14

INVITATION 14

Come Along, Little One

Being with children is double magic and double tenderness.

Truly, a backstage high-wire act with juice boxes!

Because really you're not just being with a child,

you're raising your Inner Child, too.

Every time you truly *see* a child, you get a glimpse of yourself.

And as you support a child, especially in the hard moments,

your Inner Child feels supported, too.

That quiet inner one who didn't always feel chosen.

Who sometimes still wonders if they count.

Who hides behind jokes or busyness or over-giving.

Who waits for someone to notice they're tired, or lonely,

or who could really use a pancake with a blueberry smiley face right now.

We often treat the Inner Child like a porcelain doll, like it's delicate and sentimental.

But let's be real: your Inner Child is fierce.

And funny. And has opinions.

When left out, they'll hijack your day. Mood swings, low energy, or sudden achey sadness... that might just be your little one inside, asking:

"Do I get to come along today?"

And in this Part of the book, we discover how you can whole-heartedly say:

"Yes! You come along today and we'll make it beautiful!"

Why Honoring the Inner Child
Is True Wisdom

In many cultures, the Inner Child has been misunderstood. We were taught to "grow up," to "get serious," to "toughen up." As if the parts of us that feel joy, wonder, playfulness, and creativity were weaknesses to overcome.

But being childlike is not a phase to overcome.
It is, in many ways, the source of our aliveness.

The Inner Child knows, without needing proof, what feels right and what feels wrong. It knows when something is beautiful,
when a moment is sacred, when a connection is real.

It is the part of us that can fall in love with a flower,
cry over a song, sense when someone is kind or dangerous,
or laugh uncontrollably at something silly.

It is the part that has not been taught to forget itself to fit in.
This is not foolishness. This is ancient wisdom, pure and undiluted.

Pablo Picasso, the groundbreaking painter who shaped modern art, understood that creativity requires returning to a childlike way of seeing. He said: "It took me four years to paint like Raphael, but a lifetime to paint like a child."

When we lose our connection to the Inner Child,
we may function, but we stop truly living.
We may succeed in the world's eyes, but inside, we wither.

Honoring the Inner Child does not mean refusing to take responsibility.
It means bringing the soul of life back into everything we do:
our work, our relationships, our learning, and our creating.

What an Integrated Inner Child Feels Like

Honoring the Inner Child doesn't mean losing ourselves in endless play or ignoring the realities of adult life. It doesn't mean being reckless, irresponsible, or silly all the time. Integration means wholeness. It means the Inner Child and the inner adult walk hand-in-hand, each bringing their gifts to life.

An integrated Inner Child shows up in quiet, powerful ways:

A heart that is full of kindness for yourself and others,
because you remember what it feels like to be small and vulnerable.

A belief in goodness that allows you to look for beauty, hope,
and wonder in a world that sometimes teaches cynicism.

The ability to slow down, to savor moments, to truly be
with the people you love.

Authenticity, the courage to be real, to laugh, to cry,
to be moved by life without apology.

Creativity and playfulness that bring the freedom to imagine, to create,
to explore new ideas with a light spirit, even in serious work.

And resilience, the ability to move through challenges without losing your
essential joy or self-trust.

Listening to your Inner Child doesn't take you away from your life's purpose.
It brings you home to it.

The Inner Child is the heart.
The Inner Adult is the hands.
Together, they build a life worth living.

Remembering the Good Moments

One way to include the Inner Child is to remember the good moments of your past. Even if your childhood had pain or gaps, there may have been small moments of joy tucked inside it... glimmers of connection, safety, play.

Perhaps someone baked cookies with you, or showed you how to use a hammer, or held your hand while crossing a busy street.

These memories matter. They are soul vitamins.
They live in your body, in your senses, and in your breath.

Hold them close. Share them with your child.
Let them ripple into today. Not to live in the past,
but to reclaim the sweetness that's always been part
of your story.

~ *Your Inner Child Welcome Dance* ~

Close your eyes and imagine or remember yourself as a child.
Now... give a little wiggle. A gentle shoulder roll. A mini head bop.
Maybe you touch your nose with your finger. Or you bounce in your seat with a smile. There is no right way to do this.
It's just a little fun movement that sends a signal across time:

"Hey sweet one. I'm here. I see you. You're coming with me today.
We'll make it fun. I love you. I've got us now."

This is your very own Inner Child Welcome Dance.

15

INVITATION 15

Becoming the Grown-Up You Always Needed

At the heart of this work is not only a way to support children, it's a path for becoming your own most faithful companion. You become the kind of presence who cheers you on when you forget your brilliance. Who says, "I see you," when you're sad or grumpy or puzzled. The kind who lovingly reminds you what you need to come back into your Zone.

You learn to sit with yourself in the same way you sit with a child who is sad, overwhelmed, or angry. You don't try to fix it or rush it away. You just stay close. You believe in your own goodness, just as fiercely as you believe in your child's.

When you practice this kind of self-companionship, you no longer abandon yourself in the hard moments. You let yourself be upset sometimes, just like you let your child be upset. That doesn't mean you act on it. And you wouldn't let your child act on it either. But you let the feeling be there. You recognize it not as a problem to solve, but as a wave to ride.

You allow yourself to be childlike. Not childish, but full of wonder.
Curious. Alive. Present.
Maybe you weren't allowed to be that once.
Maybe it didn't feel safe. But now you can give it to yourself.

This work begins with children.
And it becomes a portal back to yourself.

But why does self-love sometimes feel like the hardest thing to do? To understand, we need to turn toward what shaped us. Because before we can fully embrace our Inner Child, we must uncover what kept them hidden.

Love in All Its Shapes and Forms

We all want to love children well. To raise them right.

To guide them toward kindness, responsibility, and truth.

We want them to grow up knowing who they are, and how to care for others.

And most of us were raised by people who wanted the same.

Our parents and teachers meant well. They loved us.

They wanted us to be humble, thoughtful, good.

They wanted us to know right from wrong.

But sometimes, love was mixed with fear.

It wore the face of punishment, of shaming, silence, scolding, and pressure.

And it felt like love.

Because it came from the people who loved us.

But it also hurt.

And so it confused the heart.

How could love feel like this?

And we learned to associate love with pain.

We learned to expect tension in connection.

We learned to be good instead of honest.

We learned to obey instead of revealing what we truly needed.

This is not a judgment. This, too, is a kind of love.

a love shaped by wounds and survival.
A love that meant well, but carried unhealed cruelty within it.

A Flow Companion sees this. They honor the intention,
and they choose to go farther.
They say: "There's a different way to love and there's a different way to guide.
I will not repeat what happened to me."

Instead of punishment, we help a child understand what happened,
where they crossed a boundary, and how they can make things right.

Instead of scolding, we stay near and look for ways to repair.

Instead of assuming the child acted out of defiance,
we pause and ask... *Are they confused? Are they overwhelmed?*
Are they needing something they don't know how to ask for?

This is not permissiveness or giving up boundaries.

This is love without fear.

Guidance without shame.

And clarity without cruelty.

And when we offer this to a child,
something in us begins to heal too.
Because at last, we are learning what love really
feels like.

The Cocoon of Conditioning

Or How We Become Real

Every child inherits a cocoon, an invisible weave of beliefs, habits, and ways of seeing the world. And no matter how beautiful a childhood is, some form of this cocoon will wrap around each child.

Not as a punishment, but as a path.
Because this cocoon is not a prison.
It is part of the becoming.

Throughout life, each of us will press up against the edges of that cocoon,
challenging what we were taught,
peeling back the layers of protection,
remembering the untamed self underneath.

And as we break through, we experience the joy of liberation.

We find ourselves again. Stronger. Softer. More real.

This is the paradox: conditioning is both the challenge and the invitation.
It humbles us and it carves out compassion.

And when the environment is loving,
and when the child and your Inner Child feel safe inside the relationship,
that cocoon becomes a sacred chrysalis.

It's how we become real. Like the Velveteen Rabbit... threadbare, loved,
and glowing with something truer than perfection: love.

Shedding the Cocoon We Inherited
A Map Home to Yourself

As adults, many of us are still wrapped in the cocoon we were given in childhood. We carry patterns that once kept us safe, such as overworking, over-thinking, people-pleasing, bracing against joy or conflict. Without realizing these reactions were formed to survive a moment that has long since passed.

This Is the Way Home from Conditioning to Your Very Own Zone

It Starts with your Sacred No

At the beginning of your journey home, you might be exhausted.

Nothing makes sense anymore. Nothing feels right.

And something inside you says,

"No more."

You become aware of your conditioning, and you say no to pretending,

no to pleasing while you're hurting, no to pushing through.

This is the great awakening.

It makes space for what feels true, for unlearning, and rediscovering.

And the threads of your cocoon are already loosening.

You Connect with Your Sacred Yes

As you begin reclaiming your life force, you'll get glimpses of presence.

Moments of peace, where you slow down just enough to truly taste your coffee.

To notice your child's breath. To feel the warmth of your hands.

Here, you begin to re-enter your body.

You're not riding the carousel anymore. You're on the grass, breathing.

Then... Nervous System Regulation

Now you're actively tending to your inner weather.

You're soothing the inner war, and seeking peace.

This is where many people stop, because here, pain can rise.

Our unspoken fears, unmet needs, protective patterns,

or emotional echoes from long ago seek our attention. Some call it the shadow.

It's the parts of us that once had to hide just to feel safe.

Emotional Unraveling

Emotional unraveling happens through unexpected intense emotional or physical
reactions that are linked to your past: triggers. So often, it's our children and the
people we love the most who awaken the pain we haven't yet met in ourselves.
Their presence, their needs, their love, it stirs the hidden places inside us,
the parts that long to be seen, held, and healed.

Here's where the layers begin to melt.

Old sadness surfaces. Disappointment. Rage.

You meet them with kindness, not as obstacles to flow, but as guardians of it.

Some call it inner integration, parts work, or soul retrieval.

But no matter the name, the invitation is the same:

to bring your full self to the table, lovingly and without judgment,

to say, "You're allowed to be here too."

You cry with yourself. You mother yourself.

You lay down with yourself.

Every time you say, "I'm allowed to rest," or "I matter too"

you loosen the threads of your own cocoon.

Each emotion transmuted means life energy returning to you.

Finally... Grounded Lightness ... You're Living in Flow

Now joy doesn't feel like a sugar high.

It's not fleeting. It's woven into your bones.

You still get hurt or tired, but there's a steadiness now.
You don't lose yourself when the world shakes.
Because you've met the depths. You're anchored.

Now you live with your finger on the pulse of presence.
You speak from the still place.
You make decisions from inner knowing, not the mind's panic.

And yes... it takes time.
Not because flow is hard.
But because we were taught to abandon ourselves.

Coming home takes gentleness.
It takes honoring the full spiral, not forcing a shortcut.

There are many layers.
And you will walk them with grace.

No one gets to skip the dance of becoming.
And some of us... we get to dance and play and heal with children.

And the children in your care will feel it.
Because now you're grounding in yourself. And that energy is contagious:
it gives children permission to stay close to their own inner knowing too.

Little by little, the cocoon unravels.
This is how you reclaim your freedom
and finally you hear your own unique song.

When You Offer Yourself What You Need

As you begin to offer yourself the love and presence you always needed, the old patterns that once kept you small start to loosen their grip. This quiet revolution often begins not in grand gestures, but in simple, brave moments of turning toward yourself.

In the next two Invitations, we'll take a first glimpse at what this healing journey might look like. We'll explore the Sacred No, and the intergenerational repair that begins when we say: It Ends With Us.

16

INVITATION 16
Your Sacred No

Many of us learned that saying no was selfish. That to be loved, we had to stay agreeable. But always saying yes doesn't make you more generous.
It makes you more ghost.

And yet, swinging to the other extreme doesn't feel right either. You don't have to say no all the time. You are part of a living, breathing web, a family, a community, a world. You're not a "people-pleaser" when you show up for someone else's need. That's called being a parent, a friend, a companion. It's called belonging.

But when the giving becomes chronic, when the yes becomes empty,
and when it costs you your presence, your health, your joy,
then your Sacred No becomes the most generous act of all.
Because it protects something holy: your own aliveness.

Dare to say no, not in anger, not in fear but in reverence for your own becoming.
The Sacred No is not a withdrawal from love.
It's a reclamation of love that includes you, too.

Because when you feel resourced, you don't have to force patience.
It flows from you. And you don't have to pretend to be calm. You are calm.

The Sacred No isn't just a tool for parenting or teaching.
It's the foundation for living in alignment with yourself.

Your Inner Child needs you to say no to what is hurting you.
They watch not only how you speak, but how you treat yourself,
how you let others treat you, and what you tolerate in your life.

Your Inner Child doesn't want you to betray yourself to be liked.
It wants you to be safe, to be real, and to be happy.

Setting boundaries is how you become the loving guardian
your younger self perhaps did not always have.

You'll Feel It in Your Body

Something changes in your body when you say your Sacred No. You may not feel stronger right away. You may feel shaky, uncertain, or even in grief. Because saying no to something you love, something that once felt good or safe, requires more energy than saying yes.

But when you say no...truthfully, lovingly, clearly, even through tears, even while your heart is still reaching, your spine remembers. Your energy, which had been leaking out into what doesn't serve you, comes home.
You begin to feel your own flow again and reorganize your inner life around what's real for you. And that strength you start feeling...that's integrity.
That's you, having your own back.

The Art of Right Distance

The Sacred No doesn't necessarily mean cutting people out. More often, it's about finding the right kind of closeness. When someone cannot meet you with respect in the moment, the most loving thing you can do is pause. Step into the hallway. Take a breath. If you can, call in a Flow Companion, a neighbor, an elder, a trusted friend, so you can tend to your own regulation. Give both of you a moment to reset. Keeping your own behavior respectful when others cannot is an act of strength, and sometimes the only way to bring respect back into the space.

Reclaiming Yourself

So many of us have memories... just moments.

A passing comment, a single look, a teacher's shrug, a peer's laughter.

Maybe someone said, "You're not a good writer," or "Don't sing so loud," or "That's not for you."

One tiny sentence that slipped under your skin
and slowly began to diminish your trust in yourself.

Maybe you never sang again.
Maybe you didn't dance.
Maybe you still don't believe you're a leader,
or an artist, or someone whose ideas matter.

But these moments do not get to define you.
Now your Sacred No is needed to reclaim your inner space.

You are not made of other people's projections.
You are made of something far more mysterious, alive, and true.

And the real journey, the one we're on now, is reclaiming *all* that you are.

Finding the places where you stopped believing in yourself and saying:
"No. I'm going to find out for myself what is true for me."

Now you get to become the one who sees your light.
The one who sings anyway.

The Sacred Yes

Three Movements

Part 1 The Search

There is something that calls you forward.

You've felt it, beneath the noise, beneath the obligations,

beneath the version of you that learned to want the "right" things.

It is not loud. It does not argue. But it persists.

One day, you notice it. Not the thing you're supposed to want.

The thing you actually do.

A pull. A quiet insistence. So small you could ignore it,

so faithful you never really can.

This is your Sacred Yes.

Not a slogan. Not a productivity tool.

A living compass inside you. Your original direction.

You might not find it all at once. You circle it. You lose it. You taste it again.

You listen badly, then a little better. You say tiny Yeses and watch where they lead.

This is the search: learning to recognize what is truly yours

beneath what was given to you.

Part 2 What the Sacred Yes Does to You

When you begin to trust this Yes,

you stop treating yourself like a problem to be fixed.

You no longer demand a polished version of you who has it all figured out.

You come home to the mystery

to the surprise of who you are becoming,

moment by moment.

You walk with yourself in reverence, like Whitman on the open road.

You realize: you are not a project. You are a miracle unfolding.

You start saying Yes to your quirks,

to your timing, to your way of learning.

Yes to your pain and your joy.

Yes to the child you once were

and the grown-up you are now.

Yes to not knowing. Yes to trying.

Yes to failing and still being worthy of love.

Your life stops being just a linear biography, a story about getting it right.

It becomes a string of luminous moments.

You don't know what the next one will bring,

but you know who you'll meet there: yourself, anew, again and again.

Your wishes, old and new, are no longer distant fantasies.

You begin to fulfill them in small, honest ways.

And when the world doesn't understand,

when stories don't end "well," you are less shaken.

Others are allowed their opinions, their No, their endings.

You are allowed your own Yes.

Because the people who stay, the answers that arrive,

the solutions you grow,

they are yours.

Grown from your lived experience.

From your joy and your sorrow.

From your letting go and your rebuilding.

This is you, here and now,

glowing with something truer than perfection: love.

This is a homecoming, and not the last one.
You will arrive again and again, at deeper layers,
always bringing more of yourself along.

Part 3 Turning Toward the Child

And then, you look up. There is a child in front of you.
You recognize something immediately, because you have begun to recognize it
in yourself: that particular aliveness. That quiet pull toward something no one
taught them to want. The way they linger with a shell, a rhythm, a number, a
thread of story. The way their whole body says Yes before they have words for it.
This is their Sacred Yes.
Their compass. Their original direction.

Now your work changes. It becomes reverence.
Not to override it. Not to redirect it into what is convenient, measurable, or
impressive. Not to mistake their unfolding for a problem to be solved.

You become a protector of this inner compass.
You create spaces where it can breathe.
You offer materials, time, and boundaries that honor its pace.

You listen when their body says "I'm not ready yet,"
as carefully as when it says "more, more, more of this."

You remember what it cost you to betray your own Yes,
and you quietly decide: Not with this child. Not on my watch.

Allow it, and you will both be free.
Because there is nothing more exhilarating
than watching someone live from their spark,
and knowing your presence helped protect it.

This is the work. This has always been the work.

17

INVITATION 17

It Ends With Us

Healing Between the Generations

Some stories run through families like invisible patterns of pain, protection, and longing. But every cycle, no matter how old, can be transformed. You can become the turning point where old pain meets new possibility. It ends with us. Healing begins with each small choice we make today.

Sometimes, when you spend time with loved ones, and follow your Sacred Yes or Sacred No, you will encounter old pain, triggers, or sudden waves of emotion. These are signs that deeper stories are ready to be seen and healed. Often, these aren't just your own.... the beliefs and wounds that surface may have been passed from one generation to the next.

The way you meet these moments can be an act of healing, not only for you, but for everyone who came before and everyone who comes after.

This is the real work of authenticity: honoring the light, but also meeting the shadows with love.

As we move forward, we'll explore how triggers can become invitations for transformation, and how your healing is a gift that ripples through your family, your children, and beyond.

The Planet of Puzzle Hearts

~ A Story of Intergenerational Healing ~

On a strange little planet where the sky changed color with feelings
and laughter made flowers bloom out of the soil,
there lived a group of grown-ups with very unusual hearts.

Each grown-up wore their heart outside their body,
glowing like a lantern.
But it wasn't whole. Their hearts had holes.

Odd shapes scattered all across them...triangles, arrows, half-stars,
and tiny broken moons. No one knew exactly how the holes got there.

Some said they were the result of growing up.
Others whispered they were survival maps, carved when love had to be earned
or emotions hidden away. Whatever the reason, every grown-up had them.

Then came the children.

The children on this planet were wild, radiant. They didn't follow the rules of
smallness. They were loud, intense, honest. And unknowingly,
they carried puzzle pieces... shaped to fit the holes in the grown-ups' hearts.

And every time the children laughed too loud, cried too hard,
asked too many questions, refused to sit still, or loved too freely,
they were offering a puzzle piece, to fill a hole in a grown-ups heart.
The grown-ups didn't always recognize the offering,
Because, often, when the child came too close with one of those pieces,
It hurt, and their heart would flare up.

Old pain would rush in. Anger rose.
Grief, long forgotten, burst forward.
Memories flared like sparks.

And many grown-ups, overwhelmed by the sudden emotion,
pushed the child away.
The piece fell. The hole remained.

Sometimes, it grew deeper.

But one day…maybe by grace, maybe by tired surrender, the grown-ups paused.

They didn't push the children away.

They took a breath, and they let the piece come close.
They let it touch the holes in their hearts.
And yes… it stung. It wasn't easy.

And as tears came, something beautiful happened.
The children's pieces began to melt… slowly into the adults' hearts.
The more pieces they welcomed, the more their hearts began to warm.
They glowed like little suns tucked just under the skin.

And strangely, the hearts and the mouths were connected.
Because every time a grown-up smiled and breathed through the moment,
the heart grew a little bigger.
And with every smile, the glow grew warmer.
Until eventually… the hearts weren't just mending… they were expanding!

And some hearts became so spacious, that when a child offered a piece that
didn't quite fit, it simply bounced off the grown-up's heart
and returned back to the child.

And the most miraculous thing?
The piece found its way into the child's own heart,
slipping into a space that hadn't yet become a hole.
Filling something that was still forming.
Healing it before it ever had to hurt.

And the children?
They were no longer carrying pain forward.
They were carrying light.

Triggers Are Doorways to Healing

Sometimes it feels like your child, your student, or young friend,
knows exactly how to push your buttons. And you're not wrong... they do.

It's like they were born with a secret manual just for you.
They find every edge, and say the one thing that breaks the dam.
And it's not because you or they are doing anything wrong.

It's because there is something so right about this moment.
You are not just tending to a child.
You are being raised by this relationship, too.

This is the healing cycle of generations: A child activates the exact places where
you were once hurt or shut down, or forced to adapt in order to survive.
And when that button gets pushed,
and you feel the wave of discomfort rise... that's the first turning point.
You can name it for your child, so it's clear what's happening,
and they are already less scared:

 "I'm feeling really upset right now.
Let's both take a deep breath."

Then you can turn inward for just a second, hug yourself,
and say to your Inner Child:

"It's okay to feel this way. You didn't do anything wrong. We're safe and you're
not alone. I'm here with you and now we're doing it differently."

Even just saying that to your younger self, even just knowing
this is what's happening, can begin to shift everything.
Because the more awareness you bring to what's happening underneath the
surface, the more choice you have in how you respond.

Your child is here to help you rewrite your past.
You're healing the old story as you write a new one.
And in that process, both you and your child are being set free.

After a moment of trigger and loud emotion, help both yourself and your child come back to safety: notice your bodies, sip some water, share a snack, offer a grounding hug, or rest for a moment.

When you both feel steadier, it's time to imprint a new memory using the Art of Repair described in Invitation 13. Come together and peacefully talk about what happened. Create a space safe enough, to honestly talk about what happened, and share intentions to do better next time. This sequence of rupture, regulation, and repair becomes the memory that anchors deepest in a child and the medicine that transforms you as well.

The deeper layers of your own healing happen away from your child, in moments where you feel resourced enough to revisit your past; on your own, with practices like EFT (Emotional Freedom Technique), or with a skilled therapist. As you heal in those private, supported spaces, you grow the capacity to stay present and kind in difficult moments.

In every moment where you listen instead of react, where you notice instead of numb, you are healing your lineage.

~ Safe Things to Say
When Things Start Feeling Unsafe ~

Sometimes, one loving sentence can be all it takes to reconnect. Let one another feel that you're still in this together.

• "Okay, this moment is bananas. Should we take a few minutes time-out together and let it be for now and just breathe?"

• "Let's hit the reset button. You can push it on my nose."

When words are safe and hearts stay open, and even the wildest moments can become bridges back to one another.

Pain Makes You Real ~ Flow Makes You Alive

The journey of healing early wounding and shedding the cocoon of conditioning,
is where we pick up the deepest wisdom of life.

Pain makes you real. Flow makes you alive.
And together, they make you whole.

Pain cracks you open. It humbles you.
It matures your gaze so that when you speak, people listen.
When you listen, people feel seen.

And flow?
Flow is how the light pours through the cracks.
Flow is how your soul keeps dancing, even in the rubble.
It's the joy that rises not in spite of pain, but sometimes because of it,
like a wildflower that only blooms after fire.

Closing Reflection Part Five

As the cocoon of conditioning unravels, you will feel more free, happy, and empowered to create the home and life your heart desires.

As you heal the old stories, you will feel more home in your own body. You will feel held when you close your eyes and simply rest with yourself, because you can finally feel your own love standing guard.

We don't just find flow; we create the spaces for it to find us: within ourselves, in our home and all around us. Because this sacred works can truly ground in environments where everyone feels safe, relaxed, and inspired.

Let's look at the many ways we can invite this flow into our lives.

PART SIX

Flow Spirals Outward

Flow is the current of life that begins at the very center of your being and ripples outward. From the very first breath, flow guides you as you navigate the journey into the body. It is a force that carries you, unfolding its own joyfully mischievous plan, always nudging you toward more joy and freedom.

In this Part, we'll explore what it means to truly arrive in your own skin and bones. To find your anchor in the rhythm of your breath and movement.

Then, the current pulls us further, into the spaces we call home. You'll discover how to create places that don't just hold your things, but hold your spark. Places where grown-ups and children alike can shed their roles and get into the Zone.

But the current doesn't stop at the front door. The spiral keeps widening, flowing out into the streets and the heart of the community. We'll dive into the vibrant rhythm of Flow Sundays, where the village comes alive. You'll see how a shared state of play can dissolve the walls between us, creating a world where we thrive together.

From the pulse in your veins to the life in your neighborhood... the current is moving. Let's see where it takes us.

18

INVITATION 18
The Journey Into the Body

Long before a child learns to read or tie their shoes, something more profound is unfolding: the mysterious process of becoming embodied.

Children are not just growing up; they are arriving.
Into sensation. Into movement.
Into gravity, breath, emotion, and presence.

From the outside, it may look like wobbly steps, tantrums, cartwheels, giggles, wild restlessness, or hours lost in focused play.

But on the inside, something intricate is happening:
the nervous system is coming online,
the bones are hardening,
the breath is finding rhythm.
The self is meeting the body.

When we recognize this deeper journey of childhood, we start to orient differently. We don't rush to get children "ready" for life.
We create the kind of life that meets them where they are.

We become students of the body, too. And in walking beside our children,
we remember how to come home to our own.

Becoming Embodied: The Child's Deep Work

From the very beginning, our growth is not random;
it is purposeful, rhythmic, and wise.

When we are born, our movements are uncoordinated. Our bodies are here, but we haven't yet fully arrived within them. As babies, we spend our days in self-guided learning, gradually discovering how to move, how to coordinate our limbs,
how to align our will with our body.

We begin to feel where our arms are in space, how our feet carry us,
what our breath does when we cry. And with time, if we're given the space to move, rest, play, our whole system begins to come online.

In infancy, our bones are mostly soft cartilage. As we grow, the cartilage gradually ossifies, turning into strong, supportive bone:
the body literally grows into its own support system.

In parallel, the nervous system matures, the immune system calibrates,
the proprioceptive sense sharpens.
We work continuously to integrate body and mind. Everything calls us toward it. Everything wants to be touched, tasted, climbed on, explored in order to bring body and mind into harmony.
This is the deep work of childhood.

Embodied Teenagers

This journey of embodiment unfolds well into the teenage years and beyond. In adolescence, the hunger for sensory exploration may ease, as social connection takes center stage.

There's a different quality to social life when teenagers have been supported in staying connected to themselves physically.

We've seen this in our schools.

There's a self-trust, even in the midst of awkwardness, even as new emotions swirl. This doesn't mean they have no insecurities or never wobble. But the doubts don't cut as deep. The anxiety doesn't shake them as much.

They bounce back more quickly.
Because they have something to bounce back onto.

They are connected to the steady support of their bones, the hug of their connective tissue, the living memory of flow state in their own body.

Their sense of self is anchored, not in approval, but in their very skeleton. Just as their bodies are one-of-a-kind, so too are the perspectives, insights, and skills they now bring into the world.

This is why embodiment is the often-overlooked foundation of a healthy identity and resilience. When a child grows up supported in fully inhabiting their body, they carry that self-trust into their social lives, into learning, into every challenge.

The body becomes home. A safe place to return to.
The quiet, living support that holds them, always.

The Ongoing Journey of Embodiment

For most of us, the journey of embodiment unfolds into adulthood and beyond.

We may think we're embodied simply because we move, dress, or exercise our bodies, but true embodiment runs deeper. It isn't about perfect breath or posture. It's about meeting yourself where you are, again and again, in honest relationship with your living body.

Alignment does not mean your body is performing at its peak, free of pain or limitation. It means *you are with* your body, present to what is actually happening in it, in this moment, without the added weight of resistance or denial. The body is on a journey far more complex and mysterious than we can put into words, moving through seasons of openness and contraction, vitality and challenge, in ways that follow their own deep intelligence. To be in alignment is to travel with that journey rather than against it. To accept, with as much grace as you can find, whatever is unfolding. You can be completely in alignment while living with cancer, while healing from injury, while carrying the residue of deep trauma. Alignment is not the absence of difficulty. It is the quality of your presence within it.

How Do We Re-Join the Process of Embodiment?

Most of all by meeting our needs: eating and resting enough so the body can rely on regular replenishment, moving when the urge arises, and caring for the body's comfort and rhythms.

Fresh air, sunshine, bathing, and letting your mind, your awareness map your body, so you know exactly where you are in space.

Allowing your body to move on its own terms, letting it take over in dance, drumming, or any movement in flow.

When you connect in these ways, the body finds its own way to balance, and the breath naturally deepens.

When you keep meeting your genuine needs, the body realizes it's not alone.
Like a child relaxing when a loving parent takes care of them.

From this place of companionship, the body will begin to trust your invitations to relax into the Forever Now. And now, you're aligned.

Children help us remember this. They live what they feel, and in doing so, show us how to be whole. That's one of the miracles of being in the Zone with a child: their presence invites ours, not just mentally, but somatically.

They help us come home to the warm, sentient body
we so often forget we live in.

Embodiment is Empowerment

When you stop living from the neck up and start living from the whole of you, your embodiment becomes empowerment. You begin to feel safe in your body, whatever its abilities, even with painful places, and that safety grows into self-trust, regulation, and inner authority.

1. You stop gaslighting yourself.

When you live in your head, it's easy to override what your body is telling you. You push through. You ignore the tension. You tell yourself you're "fine" when you're not. But when you're embodied, you start hearing your truth earlier. You feel the "no" sooner. You start honoring your yes, your fatigue, your hunger, your grief. You become honest with yourself.

2. You make better decisions.

Embodiment gives you a built-in compass. You can feel when something's off, and you stop needing to rationalize it. The job offer that makes your gut twist? That's a no. The person who seems "perfect on paper" but your whole chest tightens around? You walk away. The yes doesn't come from your mind...it comes from resonance.

3. You regulate faster.

You notice tension rising and know how to meet it. You cry when you need to, shake when you need to, rest when you need to. You ride the waves instead of getting knocked over. This doesn't mean you're always calm. It means you're resilient.

4. You become less programmable.

You don't buy every fear-based story. You're not as easily seduced by urgency or scarcity. You're harder to manipulate. You're harder to distract. You're harder to sell nonsense to. Because you're here. In your body. On Earth. Awake.

5. *You feel pleasure again.*

Not performative pleasure. Not pleasure staged for Instagram. But subtle, earthy joy. The coziness of your couch. The way your belly feels after warm soup. The deep sigh after releasing a muscle you didn't know you were clenching. Life becomes textured again.

6. *You come home to yourself.*

Not the self you perform. Not even the one you understand.

You drop beneath all of that… into the mystery.

Into the aliveness that breathes you.

Embodiment is about experiencing yourself as a magical, cosmic being

… part of the stars, the soil, the great unfolding. It's a remembering:

I am more than I can ever think. I am part of everything.
I cannot wrap my mind around myself, I can only be myself.

This is your power.
This is your Zone.

Every Body Needs a Place

If life is a journey of embodiment, then we must ask: Where does the body get to rest? Where does it get to move freely, to stretch, to create, to release the day? Where does it get to feel unhurried, unjudged, and alive?

Flow does not float above the body. It moves through it.

So as we turn the page to the next Invitation, we are not designing places to manage activities. We are preparing places where bodies can regulate, express, and return to themselves.

Because when the body has a place, flow can find it.

19

INVITATION 19
A Place to Return To

Every body, whether a child or a grown-up, needs a place where they feel totally at ease: a little sanctuary of their own, where they call the shots. That kind of place has no expectations. No pressure to be "on," just you, doing what restores you.

Many creative people, from artists to entrepreneurs, keep a flow practice that helps them stay grounded. It's not the output they're after, but the peace that comes from disappearing into something they love.

Taylor Swift bakes bread to keep her mind steady. J.K. Rowling gardens; she says digging in the dirt helps her stay sane. Jon Stewart carves dressers, and in a podcast with Trevor Noah, he shared:

"These kinds of projects help me disappear for hours. There's a kind of peace in it. And when you come out of it, it's not as if the benefit evaporates. It stays with you. It keeps you in a grounded state."

Maybe you and your child already know this place…the one where time disappears and something inside you relaxes.

It might be as simple as a preparing a beautiful meal in your beloved kitchen, walking your favorite nature trail, or time with your journal. And as for your child, maybe they love their basket with stuffies, a play kitchen, or a blanket draped over two chairs becoming a hideaway. Perhaps, even an art table, a treehouse, an

indoor tent, where you both can hang out together or create side by side.
These are places made for the Zone.

But so often, when responsibilities press in and schedules fill, this is the first thing we sacrifice: the space where we remember who we are.
And yet, this is the space that keeps us steady.
Where the nervous system settles and the self reappears.
Sometimes even twenty unhurried minutes can restore something essential in you or your child.

Sometimes, you might share this space with a child. Other times, each of you needs time alone in your favorite place. Both matter. Both are forms of love.

Over time, returning to the same chair, corner, or table becomes its own quiet ritual. Your body starts to recognize the pattern: "Oh, this is where we get to exhale." Regular visits lay down a kind of muscle memory of safety and enjoyment, so that just walking toward this place begins to shift your nervous system into "reward time."

Flow loves this kind of steady tending. Consistency and a familiar place keep calling you back, reminding you to come home.

This is the practice: find or create a place, go there regularly, and let yourself be surprised by what arises from the core of your being.

Sharing the Joy of Flow

The beauty of the Zone is that it belongs entirely to you, or for that matter, to your child. If your magic stays hidden in your heart or on a tucked-away page, that's enough, these are *your* golden moments.

But other times, the joy overflows...as it does so often for children of all ages. They draw a picture and rush to show it. They call you to watch their cartwheel, their mudpie, their new dance. For them, sharing is part of the joy.

Sharing yours or your child's results, your music, your art, your masterfully solved puzzles, can be a way of connecting with others. If it delights you, share what you created, play a song, host a small art show, or let someone taste your home-made pasta.

You might even take your artistry to stages, competitions, and galleries, perhaps even make it your profession, and hopefully getting generously compensated, too. Because sharing that "gold medal" moment isn't about ego; it's about human excellence. It's saying,
"Look at what we humans can do when we are in flow!"
It's a gift of inspiration to everyone watching.

Whether you or your child share it with one person, your friends, or a stadium, let your artistry guide you forward on the spiral of your life.

So often, when that spiral touches another heart, something alchemical happens: the space between you wants to bloom. You begin to imagine rooms, corners, even park benches, that invite everyone, whatever their age or stage, to step into the same current of presence, and share in the delight.

This impulse ushers us into our next exploration:
How can we create flow places that bridge people
of different generations, cultures, skills, and abilities.

The Zone is Ageless

Where Generations Meet

Wherever people gather, at home, in a classroom, in a corner of a café, in a playspace or a waiting room, and whenever you have stewardship over a space, you can cultivate pockets of the Forever Now, and even flow state.

In a world that often divides people by age, skills, and role, these spaces create a different kind of belonging, a bridge between our differences.

Think of each space as an ecosystem that keeps its balance when people find what they need. The place itself invites: "Here, sip some water. Flip through this book. Tackle a puzzle. Bounce on the trampoline. Relax in this chair."

Some spots are made for solo focus and daydreams; others invite to joint creation. Each space invites a different kind of flow. When everyone finds their yes-place, peace settles in and harmony ripples out.

Four Kinds of Flow Places for All Ages

On the next pages you'll find ideas to create places for the four expressions of flow we explored in Part One:

1. A Sanctuary for Stillness Flow
2. A Studio for Creative Expression Flow
3. Open Floor Space for Movement Flow
4. Tables and Chairs for Mind Flow

To make these spaces work for everyone, provide mixed-size seating: tiny stools, floor cushions, and full-height chairs. When a toddler, a teen, and a grandparent all see a seat that fits them, they all feel equally welcomed to stay.

1. Sanctuaries of Stillness Flow

Here the body can rest and you feel the Forever Now.

Whether it's at home, in a public library, a waiting room, a café, a spa, or a garden, stillness can be invited and shared.

Indoors, a soft rug with generous pillows becomes a landing place for bodies and minds. This is a cozy corner for young and old: a place for sharing stories, reading aloud, writing a line of poetry, or simply gazing out the window.

Low shelves hold picture books, poetry, novels, and blank journals within easy reach. A warm lamp, perhaps even a candle, and armchairs or sofas offer seating that feels like an embrace. Here conversations drift in and out between paragraphs, and comfortable silence is welcome too. This shared nook supports reflection, imagination, and friendship.

Outdoors, a peaceful spot beneath a tree or a peaceful garden path invites people to settle into the quiet rhythm of nature. A shaded corner becomes an open-air living room for all ages. A bench with cushions, a small table for tea, or a hammock swaying in the breeze can turn a simple patch of earth into a sanctuary.

Nearby flowers and herbs such as mint, rosemary, roses, and lavender may release their scent when brushed by passing hands. Here conversations deepen, ideas ripen slowly, and presence feels wide and breathable.

2. Studios for Creative Expression Flow

Whether at home, at school, in summer camps, in public art and pottery studios, in museums, galleries, and makerspaces,
this is the land of "What if?" and "Let's try!"

Indoors, a maker table or art studio becomes a sanctuary for the curious, the dreamers, and the storytellers. Hands move while thoughts unwind. This is a place where the "Sacred Yes" leads the way.

A maker space and art table stocked with art supplies and loose parts such as crayons, watercolors, foil, shells, pebbles, beads, string, yarn, tape, and recycled treasures. It's a place where no one asks, "What is it?" and no one has to know. The process is the point.

Mess is sacred here. Mistakes are just movement.

For small spaces, a portable studio can live on a rolling cart or tray,
ready to appear whenever inspiration calls.

Outdoors, creativity spreads easily across a picnic table, a garden bench, or a patch of grass. A basket of simple materials such as chalk, sticks, leaves, clay, fabric scraps, can turn nature itself into a studio.

Children and adults may weave crowns of flowers, build tiny villages from stones, sketch the changing sky, or paint with water on warm pavement. In the open air, imagination stretches its wings, and creation becomes play.

3. Open Floor Space for Movement Flow

Here the body is allowed to be fully alive.

Indoors, movement flow can unfold in a playspace, a yoga studio, an adventure playground, a climbing hall, a gym...all places that naturally invite movement, exploration, and curiosity.

In smaller spaces, an open patch of floor can become a dance stage, a tumbling ground, or a quiet stretching corner. Children might naturally start to role play here, especially if there's a stage to perform on.

A yoga ball, crash pad, or balance board invites movement without instruction. If possible, a swing or hammock from the ceiling adds rhythm and delight. Weighted pillows, medicine balls, and resistance bands offer grounding input for bodies of every age.

Music belongs here too: drums, shakers, bells, rhythm sticks, or a xylophone, anything that can be tapped, shaken, strummed, or stomped. Music isn't background in this space; it is active play. It is joy made audible.

Outdoors, movement finds its natural playground. A grassy field, a climbing tree, a sandy beach, or a path along a river invites running, balancing, leaping, and exploring.

Logs become balance beams.
Hills become slides.
Stones become stepping paths.

In the open air, bodies rediscover their ancient conversation with gravity, rhythm, and space.

4. Tables and Chairs for Mind Flow

Here, the mind gets to play.

Indoors, a table becomes a gathering place for deep focus and joyful challenge. Children and adults can spread out board games, dive into puzzles, or build intricate imagination landscapes with blocks and figurines.

This is the place for Sudoku, jigsaw puzzles, math challenges, and strategy games. The satisfaction of the "aha!" moment.

Surround the space with science, art, and history books, those thick, beautiful volumes that allow us to travel the world without leaving our chair. Blank journals and big paper invite maps of ideas, inventions, and daydreams.

Outdoors, the thinking mind wakes up differently. A table on a porch, a bench in a park, or a blanket spread beneath a tree can become a place for reading, sketching, journaling, or contemplating.

Children might collect leaves and sort them like scientists, draw what they observe, or invent stories about clouds drifting overhead. Here the mind stretches outward, carried by curiosity and the wide horizon of the world.

From the logic of a puzzle to the freedom of imagination, this is where we map our inner worlds.

The Three Flow Agreements

These agreements, whether written down or shared aloud as often as needed, invite a spirit of safety, respect, and freedom:

1. Treat Materials with Care

Paintbrushes, books, instruments, microscopes, and the like are treasures to be handled kindly. Mistakes or mishaps are part of learning; when something spills or breaks, we reset together and begin again.

2. Return Things to Their Place

When an activity ends, materials return home. Order makes the next spark of inspiration easier to follow. Tidying up is not a chore; it's the natural closing of the experience, best done together.

3. Honor Each Other's Flow

When someone is deeply engaged, pause before interrupting. Ask before joining. Sometimes we flow together, sometimes side by side, sometimes alone. If energy grows loud or wild, we simply shift to a space where everyone can thrive.

A nice addition may be adding signage in simple language: Tiny cards with "Take a cushion; linger as long as you like" reduce the need for verbal direction and empower shy visitors.

These simple agreements *tune* the room. Post them on a card, model them in your gestures, and offer reminders when necessary, and they will weave an invisible net of safety. Everyone learns what kindness looks like, where treasures belong, and how to honor another's absorption. Within this field of agreements, minds can rest and hearts can roam. The space settles into a rhythm, ready for all to play in the Zone together.

Flow, Belonging, and Our Shared Lives

Flow shapes how we belong...to ourselves and to one another.
When we enter the Zone together, something subtle shifts. Laughter softens edges. Attention deepens. The nervous system relaxes in company. We begin to feel the joy of sharing presence in the Forever Now.

When enough people gather in that spirit, something new becomes possible...

As a parting gift, in the last chapter of this book, I want to share a vision
that is very dear to my heart, a practical experiment in community:
Flow Sundays.

Let's explore how we might bring the magic of the Zone into our shared lives.

20

INVITATION 20
Flow Sundays
Creating Rhythms For Community

I've seen this everywhere, all over the world. Beneath the schedules, solo dinners, and group chats, there is a wish to raise children within a circle.

This wish isn't just in parents. It lives in elders who long to be needed, in neighbors who miss the sounds of childhood, in adults who wonder where their own circle went, and in people without children who would love to belong somewhere real.

There's a wish to share soup and stories.
To let children run free in a space that feels safe, because we made it so.
To know that when your child cries, another pair of kind eyes is also watching.
To know you don't have to hold it all alone.

Creating this kind of community is not easy in today's fast, fragmented world.
But Flow Sundays might be a way to do it.

They offer children the experience of seeing their grown-ups relax and laugh together as they do meaningful things. And they offer grown-ups a chance to feel less alone in the daily work of raising children.

They also answer something deeper: everyone's greatest wish.

Fulfilling Our Greatest Wish

Underneath our desires, most of us, whether child or grown-up,
have a simple wish:

Please, see me. Please let me be me.

Not who you think I should be. Not who you wish I was. But me. The real me.

We can do that for one another in relaxed places
and most of all we can do it for children:

So much of what we call misbehavior is really just the cry of an unseen child,
a child squeezed into expectations that were never meant for them.

At Flow Sundays, we gather to truly see the child in front of us. We let go of the
scripts. We notice who they really are...what lights them up, what calms them,
what sparks their flow.

This small shift can change so much.
When a child feels seen, they settle and they shine.
Most of all, they stop fighting for scraps of attention.
They realize: *I belong. I am welcome. I am safe to be me.*
And this ripples outward and inward. It creates a field where the Inner Child
 in every adult feels one step closer to be seen.

Flow Sundays is not a program. Not a playdate. It's an experiment in
community...

A Door Opens. You Step Inside.

You're not quite sure what to expect, but the door is open, and that already feels
like an invitation. Inside, the pace is slower, and there's a warmth that says,
"Ah, you're here. We've been waiting for you."

Some people are already settled. A few children are sprawled on the floor, arranging flowers in little vases. In the corner, a basket of wooden toys sits like a pile of possibilities. Nearby, a father and daughter are exploring a shelf of instruments, maybe a kalimba or a drum, testing the sounds like they're discovering a new language.

Someone's sitting nearby, folding paper in silence, and a child wanders over to ask, "What are you making?" Just like that, connection begins.

There's no schedule; this afternoon is timeless. You might find yourself at a table cutting shapes beside someone new, or discovering that you actually know how to play a xylophone. You might end up lying on your back in the backyard, watching a child make up a story about clouds, or simply sitting on the edge of the room, doing absolutely nothing. No one will mind.

Sometimes there's a circle to share names, interests, small truths.
"I love paper snowflakes."
"I just moved here."
"I brought this game I used to play as a kid."
From there, the day unfolds itself.

This is Flow Sunday.
For a few hours, a living room becomes a village. A backyard becomes a commons. And a box of watercolors becomes a bridge between two strangers.
It's not about doing everything...just finding the next little yes. And letting that be enough.

This is how community reimagines itself.
One open door at a time.

One moment of flow at a time.

A Seed for Community

A Flow Sunday is a gathering with a purpose: to share time and space with children, and to catch a glimpse of what village life could feel like. It's an invitation to being present together. Here are the core pillars of Flow Sundays:

Children & Flow at the Center

This isn't one of those parties where the adults retreat to a "grown-up island" while the kids are playing at the sidelines. It's about *being with* the children, connecting with them, and sometimes finding flow alongside them.

It's not about directing children, nor disappearing. Instead, Flow Sundays create a shared social field where both children and adults bring what interests them, allowing inspiration to move freely between generations.

Children may lead you into their world. They may want to show you something, explain a game, or invite you into their imagination. Receive them... with your eyes, your care, and your full attention. And when the moment feels right, share your own "Yes." You might offer a simple invitation to an activity that matters to you, or get absorbed in something, and see who feels drawn to join you.

Extended Family & Friends Welcome

This is a beautiful chance to include aunties, uncles, neighbors, friends, anyone who wants to build loving connection with children and others.

Three Hours

A clear beginning, middle, and end. Everyone knows it's three hours of togetherness, presence, and flow. It's enough time to dive into the mystery, but short enough not to hit that "over-stimulated" wall.

Three Zones of Engagement

    Quiet Activities: like puzzles, drawing, beading, sharing stories

    Movement Activities: dancing, fort building, ball games

    Snack & Rest Zone: because no one can flow on an empty tummy

That's a great start.

Flow Sunday... All The Things It Could Be

It could feel like a party.
But not a party with hired clowns, loud music, and sugar crashes.
A self-made party, where kids and adults invent their own joy.

It could be a sanctuary.
Where time slows down. Where children aren't rushed, graded, or corrected.
Where they're safe to unfold.

It could be a child's golden memory.
That one day a month where they feel like they truly belong.

It could be a ripple maker.
Even one Flow Sunday can change a child's life path.

It could be a family reweaver.
Restoring the threads between generations.

It could be multi-generational.
Toddlers and elders, side by side, creating and witnessing.

It could be a spark-gathering.
A monthly treasure hunt for flow: "I didn't know I loved weaving / painting /
dancing until today."

It could be a break from the achievement race.
Not about proving. Just joyful doing for the sake of being.

It could be a homecoming.
For children. For grown-ups. For Inner Children long forgotten.

A Few More Details About Flow Sundays

It doesn't have to be on Sundays.

Choose any day and time that works for your community, when you have three uninterrupted hours. Over time, your group might find its own rhythm; once a month, every season, or just when life makes space for it.

You can start small.

Three to five grown-ups and a few children is plenty. It can grow naturally as you feel safer in your offering. If you'd like to expand, you can use local tools, like community bulletin boards, parenting circles, apps like *Meetup* and *Nextdoor*, online groups, or even your child's school or extracurricular network, to find like-minded people.

You don't need a special venue.

Flow Sundays can happen in living rooms, backyards, parks, or community spaces... wherever people feel comfortable.

Consider having an online message group.

In an email or messages thread people can post what they feel like offering: "I'll bring instruments," "I can set up a crafting table," "Let's meet at my house next time." Ideally, you rotate homes and keep it collaborative.

For the gathering itself, you might include...

Any flow stations introduced in Invitation 19, that offer

– Art materials (crayons, pastels, watercolor)

– Books, puzzles, musical instruments

– A comfy corner with pillows or blankets

– Nature treasures (stones, leaves, feathers)

– A movement space or outdoor area

A few snacks. A pot of tea. A jar of flowers. Let the space feel welcoming for both children and adults.

The Three Flow Agreements

Write them on a little poster and name them in the introductory circle. Clear agreements help everyone feel safe.

1. We return things to where we found them.

2. We honor each other's flow, children's and adults'.

3. If a conflict arises, we meet it with kindness and curiosity.

Tips for grown-ups:

Follow your child's invitation.

Observe and listen without rushing to direct.

Join their play without taking over.

Icebreaker Places

Here are three places that invite first connections.

The Invitation Table.

This is a spark station for children and adults. A place where connection begins:
Set up a bowl of magical prompts printed or hand-lettered, something like:

• Find something red together.

• Make the quietest sound you can think of.

• Invent a secret handshake with someone.

The Mapping Table

Set out butcher paper, pencils, stencils, and stamps. Invite guests to draw: a map
of your dream village, a treasure map, a map of your heart today, a map of this
Flow Sunday

The Storytelling Circle

Set out a few cushions or a special chair and invite participants to tell a short story
from their lives or their imagination. You can offer prompts like stones, image
cards, or simple objects.

Flow Sundays for Older Children

As children grow, their play deepens and they need more substance. They still crave joy, connection, and freedom... but they no longer want to just play.

They want to create. They want to contribute.

They want to feel like what they do matters.

Flow Sundays for older children might look like:

- ◊ Cooking a meal for the whole group, together.
- ◊ Organizing an art gallery of their creations.
- ◊ Designing and tending a shared garden bed.
- ◊ Hosting a little neighborhood performance.
- ◊ Offering a mini booth or gift shop with handmade items.
- ◊ Organizing something meaningful, like a donation drive, a beach clean-up, or packing supplies for someone in need.

This is creativity with purpose. It's a chance for older children to experience agency, responsibility, and belonging, while still flowing, laughing, and dreaming alongside their peers and grown-up companions.

Children want to make something that counts.
And they want to do it with people who love them just as they are.

Flow Sunday
The Circle Begins and Ends

At the beginning and in the end of Flow Sundays it can be lovely to come together in a circle with whoever is already there or hasn't left yet. This is one way to anchor the group in presence, but it is entirely optional.

Some people may arrive after the circle has begun, and some may prefer just to observe. You might turn it into a simple song, or a shared moment of silence. Or you may decide to skip it altogether. Whatever feels right for each gathering.

The Circle Begins

Raise your hand to the sky.

Then, touch the ground.

Then, touch your heart, and smile at the others in the circle.

The Circle Ends

Hold your hands together like a bowl.

Raise the bowl to the sky.

Place hands back on the heart and wave good-bye to one another.

Dissolving the "Perfect Plan" in Herbal Tea

There is a moment, right before people arrive—the children, adults, family, and new friends—when your mind wants to imagine how it will go.

Who will do what... how they will respond... what they might learn.
Your brain starts narrating: "And then the children will sit in a perfect circle...and then Aunt Martha will finally understand the deep mysteries of the heart...
and then..."

This is where the ceremony begins.
Make yourself a cup of herbal tea and let your expectations dissolve
like the steam rising from your cup.

A flow place is a living field. It reveals itself only when real human beings enter with their whole, beautiful, unfinished selves.

They will meet the space with the level of safety, readiness,
and curiosity they have today.

And you as the host, you are the one who sets the tone for kindness,
to make it safe and inspiring for all.

You know the Zone.
You befriended the mystery,
You're not afraid of the absurd.

You carry your Sacred No for when things get too wild,
and your glowing Yes to encourage the vibe.
You know how to repair with grace,
you are well-equipped.

And then within the safety of your field, you can let life unfold.

As always, flow might arrive in unexpected ways.
And things that seem to go "wrong" may, in truth, be going beautifully right.

A mistake might spark laughter.
A spill might invite connection.
A moment of awkwardness might melt everyone into their shared humanity.

Flow loves surprise, and that's the most delightful part.

Sometimes, in spaces like these, people finally feel free enough
to reveal who they really are:
creative, innocent, unguarded, and wonderfully human.

Closing Reflection Part Six

Flow Learning doesn't end with this book.
It wants to become something lived
in our homes, our communities,
and in the places where we all learn and grow.

Every time you create a moment of safety,
or an environment where a child can follow their spark,
you're participating in something much larger.

These small gestures are the building blocks
of a new learning culture.
A culture where children are seen.
Where adults rediscover their own aliveness.
Where learning grows from curiosity, relationship, and joy.

You now carry the principles, the practices,
and the spirit of flow.

Whether you grow a simple home rhythm,
a neighborhood circle, or a full school or learning program
this work will meet you and guide you.

This is the beginning of a culture where children belong,
adults feel supported, and learning feels like life again.

This is your life.
This is your moment.
This is life in the Zone with your child.
Let's celebrate it.

AFTERWORD

The Story Behind the Book

I was in my mid-twenties, overwhelmed by university and the pressure to become someone. My nervous system was tight like a violin string, straining to play the perfect melody of adulthood.

When I volunteered at the International SOS Children's Villages, something shifted. Hundreds of children had access to beautifully prepared tents: tiny Montessori environments with art supplies, musical instruments, and circus props.

I was a translator and storyteller, but mostly... I had time. Time to just be with the children. I sat with them. I watched. I listened. I played a little. I followed their lead, and something in me exhaled. They were present in a way I hadn't been for years. While I had been striving and becoming... they had been *being*. For the first time in ages, I wasn't trying to fix or prove anything. I was just... me.

And somehow, on the floor of a tent, surrounded by beads and feathers and glue sticks, I felt safe. I didn't know it was called flow. I didn't know I had entered what I now call *in the Zone with your child*. I just knew something in me remembered how to breathe again. And I've followed that thread ever since.

My Path

I enrolled in a Montessori teacher training, not knowing where it would lead, only that something inside me had awakened.

There were moments of reverence. I remember the guide folding a napkin with such care... it was a lesson in grace. My breath slowed. My shoulders softened. Every movement became a meditation.

When I touched the *golden beads*, (the Montessori math material for the decimal system) something lit up inside me. Suddenly, math wasn't confusing or abstract. It was alive. Beautiful. Sacred. I realized: I was never bad at math. I was just misaligned with how it was taught. With the right tools, my mind and body sighed in recognition: "Of course, this is how it works!"

Another Wake-Up Call

One day, when I was still living in Europe, I attended a workshop with Rebeca and Mauricio Wild called in German "Erziehung zum Sein" (Education for Being.)

No PowerPoints. No lecture. Just a circle and a conversation. "We created a school in Ecuador," they said, "where children can play all day long."

They described a school that was all movement and no agenda, where children were free to play and explore, and adults only guided when they were needed for emotional safety or deeper explorations. Where "the genuine needs of the child *are* the curriculum." That sentence opened something in me that has never closed.

I heard about indoor and outdoor spaces filled with tools, instruments, books, art materials...real things for real life. They said,
"When a child's needs are met, they love to learn."
I was electrified. I had found my path.

Within a year, I volunteered at one of their inspired schools in Austria. Then I became the educational director of that school. Then I helped create a school in my hometown in Northern Italy.

It was incredibly mind and heart opening to work with children who were allowed to happily go about their day, playing, conversing, inventing, and creating as their hearts desired.
This wasn't education as I knew it. This was education as presence.
As love in motion. As the architecture of freedom.

The Deepening

But soon I realized: being present is much harder when I'm in pain.
During those seasons, I found my helpers. Sometimes in the form of friends, sometimes in practitioners and healing modalities like Feldenkrais, meditation, EFT (Emotional Freedom Technique), Pranic Healing,... and so often in books that helped with just the right words at the right time.

All of these supported me through the cancer death of my mother, the slow decline of my uncle, heartbreak after separations and losses, the passing of friends and pets, and years of knee pain.

In those moments, I turned toward the darkness inside me. I learned to be present with it. And I discovered it was not evil. It did not want to hurt me. It was a child, longing to be comforted.

My First Flow Companion

My mother was a single mom who had me later in life, in her early forties. She prepared a *Yes Environment* for me long before she ever heard the word Montessori.

I had a drawer with puzzles, a bench with art supplies, a little library of books, and even an abacus gifted by a family friend. I had toys and tools freely available to me, nobody hovering, nobody forcing. Just my presence, just space.

She subscribed me to various kid's magazines, offered me colorful pens and interesting objects, and let me explore. For years, she also drove me regularly to figure skating and music lessons, and I developed a decent skill set.

But what I remember most is how she treated me... I was a very headstrong child and we didn't always get along. I said a lot of no's. Sometimes, she would ask me, "Can you say yes, just once?" and I'd scream back, "No!"

But she didn't try to break me and she never punished me. In a way, she was kind of fascinated, maybe even amused by my emerging personality, and gave me the room I needed to feel what I needed to feel. To come back in my own time and apologize when I was ready.

And because of that, I had an experience that changed me forever:
the experience of unconditional love.
I grew up with the sense that my will was allowed to exist. That my opinion mattered and that I was supported, even when I was being difficult.

That was the greatest gift I've ever received. And it made me who I am today.

And Now... This Book Is My Gift to You

I wrote this book not because I have figured it all out, but because I needed these words, too. Every chapter was a lesson I was learning and healing in real-time, and I suspect I will always be learning and healing even more.

My hope is that you found something in these pages that makes you want to sit a little closer, breathe a little deeper, and step a little more into the Zone.

To remember what you've always known:

That magic is already inside you.

That joy is the natural shape of learning.

That your presence is your greatest gift, and as a child you gave it freely.

No matter how far you've wandered,

you can always return to the Zone.

The door is still open.

The child is still waiting.

And the rhythm of life is always singing...

Come play!

Bonus: A Final Note from Fluffy Himalayan Cat and Flow Mentor

As we come to the end, I feel it's only right to offer the last word to my most unexpected and wise teacher of flow, my cat Princess Himalayan Hope, also known as Fluffy.

If you've ever been trusted by a reserved, rescued, half-wild tiny white lion, you know: when she speaks, you listen.
So now... a few words from her.

Dear Reader,

If you've made it to the end of this book,
I want to personally congratulate you on your commitment to presence.
I know presence when I see it, because I *am* presence.

While you've been reading all these wonderful words,
I've been sitting with them too.
Literally.
I warmed them for you.
You're welcome.

This book talks a lot about flow, trust, joy, curiosity...
These are not goals for me. These are defaults.
I nap when I'm tired.
I stretch when I'm ready.
I leap when the energy says yes.
I do not overthink. I do not hustle.

And I most certainly do not chase things that aren't meant for me.
(Except the red dot. That menace must be stopped.)

This book speaks of sacred boundaries....

Sweetie, I invented sacred boundaries.

Try petting me when I don't want it and you'll learn very fast.

And one more thing...something important:

In real life, I only come close when a human is truly present...

when they are actually *here with me*.

Otherwise, I am mist, whiskers, and moonlight...gone.

So if someday you sense a tiny shift in the air,

a shimmer in the corner of your eye,

or the faintest brush against your leg...

it might be me.

I like to appear to people who are aligned and open,

even for just one breath.

It's my way of saying,

"Yes. Right here. You found the Forever Now."

Now go curl up in your life like it's a basket of sun-warmed towels.

Be gentle. Be curious.

And flow on, Darling.

Fluffy,
Your Feline Flow Companion

Bibliography

Archer, Dale. The ADHD Advantage. What You Thought Was a Diagnosis May Be Your Greatest Strength. Avery, 2015.

Aron, Elaine N. The Highly Sensitive Person: How to Thrive When the World Overwhelms You. New York: Broadway Books, 1996.

Axline, Virginia. *Dibs in Search of Self.* Boston: Houghton Mifflin, 1964.

———. *Play Theory: The Inner Dynamics of Childhood.* Boston: Houghton Mifflin, 1947.

Berger, Warren. *A More Beautiful Question: The Power of Inquiry to Spark Breakthrough Ideas.* Bloomsbury 2006.

Bonhoeffer, Jan. "How Parents and Kids Can Find Flow: How To Stop Time And Have More Fun" *Psychology Today,* Posted November, 20, 2023. Retrieved from https://www.psychologytoday.com/us/blog/heart-of-healthcare/202311/how-parents-and-kids-can-find-flow

Bowlby, John. *Attachment and Loss.* Vol. 1. New York: Basic Books, 1969.

Bradshaw, John. *Home Coming: Reclaiming and Championing Your Inner Child.* Bantam Books: New York, 1992.

Breuning, Loretta Graziano. *Habits of a Happy Brain: Retrain Your Brain to Boost Your Serotonin, Dopamine, Oxytocin, and Endorphin Levels.* Adams Media, 2016.

Brown, Stuart. *Play: How it Shapes the Brain, Opens the Imagination, and Invigorates the Soul.* New York: Penguin, 2010.

Cameron, Julia. *The Artist's Way: A Spiritual Path to Higher Creativity.* TarcherPerigee, 2002.

Campbell, Joseph. *The Power of Myth.* Edited by Betty Sue Flowers, Anchor Books, 1991.

Capacchione, Lucia. *Recovery Of The Inner Child: The Highly Acclaimed Method For Liberating Your Inner Self.* New York: Simon & Schuster, 1991

Childre, Doc & Martin, Howard. *The Heartmath Solution: The Institute of Heartmath's Revolutionary Program for Engaging the Power of the Heart's Intelligence.* New York: Harper Collins Publishers, 1999.

Choa Kok Sui. *The Ancient Science and Art of Pranic Healing.* Institute for Inner Studies, 1987.

———. *Meditations for Soul Realization: A Practical Guide for the Development of the Soul.* Institute for Inner Studies, 2000.

Chou, Ting-Jui, and Chien-Hsiung Ting. "The Flow Experience in Computer Games." Computers in Human Behavior, vol. 19, no. 3, 2003, pp. 275–294.

Claxton, Guy. *Hare Brain, Tortoise Mind: How Intelligence Increases When You Think Less*. New York: Harper Perennial, 1999.

Cohen, Lawrence. *Playful Parenting: An Exciting New Approach To Parenting That Will Help You Nurture Close Connections, Solve Behavior Problems, Encourage Confidence*. New York: Ballantine Books, 2001.

Craig, Gary. The EFT Manual. Energy Psychology Press, 2008.

Csíkszentmihályi, Mihály. *Flow: The Psychology of Optimal Experience*. New York: Harper & Row, 1990.

Csíkszentmihályi, Mihály, and Jeanne Nakamura. "Effortless Attention in Everyday Life: A Systematic Phenomenology." Effortless Attention: A New Perspective in the Cognitive Science of Attention and Action, edited by Brian Bruya, MIT Press, 2010, pp. 179–190.

———. *Creativity: Flow and the Psychology of Discovery and Invention*. New York: Harper Collins, 1996.

———. *Finding Flow: The Psychology of Engagement with Everyday Life*. New York: Basic Books, 1998.

———. *The Evolving Self: A Psychology for the Third Millennium*. New York: Harper Perennial, 2018.

Davies, Simone. *The Montessori Toddler: A Parent's Guide to Raising a Curious and Responsible Human Being*. Workman Publishing Company, 2019.

Deci, Edward & Ryan, Richard M. *Intrinsic Motivation and Self-Determination in Human Behavior*. New York: Springer, 1985.

Doczi, György. *The Power of Limits: Proportional Harmonies in Nature, Art, and Architecture*. Shambhala, 1981.

Donaldson, O. Fred. *Playing By Heart: The Vision and Practice of Belonging*. Deerfield Beach, FL: Health Communications, 1993.

Duckworth, Angela. *Grit: The Power of Passion and Perseverance*. New York: Scribner, 2016.

Durkheim, Émile. The Elementary Forms of Religious Life. Translated by Karen E. Fields, Free Press, 1995.

Elkind, David. *Child Development and Education*. New York: Oxford Univ. Press, 1976.

———. *The Power of Play: Learning What Comes Naturally*. Philadelphia: Da Capo Press, 2007.

Ericsson, K. Anders, Ralf Th. Krampe, and Clemens Tesch-Römer."The Role of Deliberate Practice in the Acquisition of Expert Performance." Psychological Review, vol. 100, no. 3, 1993, pp. 363–406.

Ericsson, K. Anders, and Robert Pool. *Peak: Secrets from the New Science of Expertise.* Houghton Mifflin Harcourt, 2016.

Feldenkrais, Moshe. *Awareness Through Movement: Health Exercises for Personal Growth.* Penguin Books, 1980.

Feldman, Ruth. "Parent–Infant Synchrony: A Biobehavioral Model of Mutual Influences in the Formation of Affiliative Bonds." Monographs of the Society for Research in Child Development, vol. 77, no. 2, 2012, pp. 42–51.

Franklin, Benjamin. *The Autobiography of Benjamin Franklin.* Edited by Leonard W. Labaree et al., Yale University Press, 1964.

Frost, Joe L., Wortham, Sue C., & Reifel, Stuart C. *Play and Child Development.* Englewood Cliffs, NJ: Prentice Hall, 2000.

Gandini, Lella, Edwards, Carolyn, Forman, George (Eds.) *The Hundred Languages Of Children: The Reggio Emilia Approach to Early Childhood Education.* Norwood, NJ: Ablex Publishing, 1994.

Gardner, Howard. *Frames of Mind: The Theory of Multiple Intelligences. New York: Basic Books, 1983.*

Gatto, John Taylor. *Dumbing us Down: The Hidden Curriculum Of Compulsory Schooling.* Gabriola Island, BC: New Society Publishers, 2002.

Gerber, Magda & Johnson, Allison. *Your Self-Confident Baby: How to Encourage Your Child's Natural Abilities from the Very Start.* New York: John Wiley & Sons, 1998.

Grandin, Temple. *Visual Thinking: The Hidden Gifts of People Who Think in Pictures, Patterns, and Abstractions.* Riverhead Books, 2022.

Gray, Peter. *Free to Learn: Why Unleashing the Instinct to Play Will Make Our Children Happier, More Self-Reliant, and Better Students for Life.* New York: Basic Books, 2013.

Henley, W. E. (1875). *Invictus.* Retrieved from Poetry Foundation: https://www.poetryfoundation.org/poems/51642/invictus

Hewlett, Barry S., and Michael E. Lamb, editors. Hunter-Gatherer Childhoods: Evolutionary, Developmental and Cultural Perspectives. Aldine de Gruyter, 2005.

Holt, John. *Learning All The Time.* New York: Da Capo Lifelong Books, 1990.

Huberman, A. (2021, September 27). Controlling Your Dopamine For Motivation, Focus & Satisfaction. Huberman Lab Podcast

Hughes, Bob. A Playworker's Taxonomy of Play Types. 2nd ed., PlayEducation, 2002.

Huizinga, Johan. Homo Ludens: A Study of the Play-Element in Culture. Routledge & Kegan Paul, 1949.

Immordino-Yang, Mary Helen, and Antonio Damasio. "We Feel, Therefore We Learn: The Relevance of Affective and Social Neuroscience to Education." Mind, Brain, and Education, vol. 1, no. 1, 2007, pp. 3–10.

Isaacson, Walter. *Einstein: His Life and Universe*. Simon & Schuster, 2007.

Jung, Carl G. Synchronicity: *An Acausal Connecting Principle.* Princeton University Press, 1973.

———. *Man and His Symbols*. Dell Publishing, 1964.

———. *The Archetypes and the Collective Unconscious*. Princeton University Press, 1981.

Kaminski, Rami. *The Gift of Not Belonging: How Outsiders Thrive in a World of Joiners.* Post Hill Press, 2024.

Kardaras, Nicholas. Glow Kids: *How Screen Addiction Is Hijacking Our Kids - and How to Break the Trance* St. Martin's Griffin 2016.

Katahira K, Yamazaki Y, Yamaoka C, Ozaki H, Nakagawa S and Nagata N "EEG Correlates of the Flow State: A Combination of Increased Frontal Theta and Moderate Frontocentral Alpha Rhythm in the Mental Arithmetic Task" *Frontiers in Psychology*, 2018. 9:300. doi: 10.3389/fpsyg.2018.00300

Keltner, Dacher. Awe: The New Science of Everyday Wonder and How It Can Transform Your Life. Penguin Press, 2023.

King, Maxwell. *The Good Neighbor: The Life and Work of Fred Rogers*. Abrams Press, 2018.

Kotler, Steven. *The Rise of Superman: Decoding the Science of Ultimate Human Performance.* New Harvest, 2014.

Knight, Sara. *Risk and Adventure in Early Years Outdoor Play: Learning from Forest Schools*. London: Sage Publications, 2011.

Kohn, Alfie. *Punished by Rewards: The Trouble with Gold Stars, Incentive Plans, A's, Praise, and Other Bribes.* Boston: Houghton Mifflin, 1993.

Kotb, Hoda. "Stop Reading Eckhart Tolle and Just Watch Your Kids as They Live in the Moment." People, 9 June 2025, pp. 28-29.

Kramer, Rita. *Maria Montessori: A Biography.* Da Capo Press, 1988.

Lansbury, Janet. *Elevating Child Care: A Guide to Respectful Parenting.* Malibu: JLML Press, 2014.

———. *No Bad Kids: Toddler Discipline Without Shame.* Malibu: JLML Press, 2014.

Lao Tzu, Stephen Mitchell (Translator). *Tao Te Ching*. Perennial Classics, 2006.

Lawlor, Robert. *Voices of the First Day: Awakening in the Aboriginal Dreamtime*. Rochester, Vermont: Inner Traditions International, 1991.

Lazenby, Roland. Michael Jordan: *The Life*. Little, Brown and Company, 2014.

Lent, Jeremy R. *The Patterning Instinct: A Cultural History of Humanity's Search for Meaning*. Amherst, New York: Prometheus Books, 2017.

Leong, Victoria, et al. "Speaker Gaze Increases Information Coupling between Infant and Adult Brains." Proceedings of the National Academy of Sciences, vol. 114, no. 50, 2017, pp. 13290–13295.

Lipton, Bruce. *The Biology of Belief: Unleashing the Power of Consciousness, Matter and Miracles*. Authors Pub Corp, 2005.

Louv, Richard. *Last Child in the Woods: Saving Our Children from Nature Deficit Disorder*. Chapel Hill, NC: Algonquin Books of Chapel Hill, 2005.

Macnamara, Brooke N., David Z. Hambrick, and Frederick L. Oswald. "Deliberate Practice and Performance in Music, Games, Sports, Education, and Professions: A Meta-Analysis." Psychological Science, vol. 25, no. 8, 2014, pp. 1608–1618.

Maturana Humberto. *The Tree of Knowledge: The Biological Roots of Human Understanding*. Boulder, Colorado: Shambala Publications, 1992.

McMillin, Jamie. *Legendary Learning: The Famous Homeschoolers' Guide to Self-Directed Excellence*. Rivers & Years Publishing LLC, 2011.

Mellin, Laurel. *Wired for Joy: A Revolutionary Method for Creating Happiness from Within*. Carlsbad, Hayhouse, 2010.

Mitchell, Stephen. *Tao Te Ching*, New York: Harper Collins, 1988.

Montessori, Maria. *The Absorbent Mind*. New York: Holt, Rinehart and Winston, 1949.

———. *The Child in the Family*. London: Pan, 1970.

———. *The Discovery of the Child*. New York: Ballantine, 1986.

———. *The Secret of Childhood*. New York: Ballantine, 1972.

Murphy Paul Annie. *The Extended Mind: The Power of Thinking Outside the Brain*. Mariner Books 2021.

Nagelhout, Ryan. "Play Helps Children Build Better Brains. Here Are Some Ways To Get Kids Learning" *Harvard Graduate School of Education Blog,* 2025.

Nelson-Isaacs, Sky. *Living in Flow: The Science of Synchronicity and How Your Choices Shape Your World.* North Atlantic Books, 2019.

Nelson, Jane. *Positive Discipline: The Classic Guide to Helping Children Develop Self-Discipline, Responsibility, Cooperation, and Problem-Solving Skills.* New York: Random House, 1981.

Neophytou, Eliana, Laurie A. Manwell, and Roelof Eikelboom. "Effects of Excessive Screen Time on Neurodevelopment, Learning, Memory, Mental Health, and Neurodegeneration: A Scoping Review." Current Psychiatry Reports, vol. 21, no. 8, 2019, pp. 1–10.

Noah, Trevor. "Meet Jon Stewart – One of My Favorite People." What Now? with Trevor Noah, season 2, episode 41, SiriusXM Podcasts / Simplecast, 12 June 2025.

Parker-Ellis Becky. "Playful Brains: Early Years Play Shapes Children's Futures" *Neuroscience News*, October 2, 2023. Retrieved from https://neurosciencenews.com/play-brain-neurodevelopment-24903/

Payne, Kim John, and Lisa M. Ross. *Simplicity Parenting: Using the Extraordinary Power of Less to Raise Calmer, Happier, and More Secure Kids.* Ballantine Books, 2009.

Pearce, Joseph C. *Magical Child: Rediscovering Nature's Plan for Our Children.* London: Paladin, 1979.

———. *Magical Child Matures.* New York: Bantam, 1983.

———. *The Crack in the Cosmic Egg: Challenging Constructs of Mind and Reality.* Park Street Press, 2002.

Pearsall, Paul. *The Hearts' Code: Tapping the Wisdom and Power of Our Heart Energy.* New York: Random House, 1998.

Peifer, Corinna, et al. "A Scoping Review of Flow Research." Frontiers in Psychology, vol. 13, 2022, article 745987.

Pestalozzi, Johann Heinrich. *How Gertrude Teaches Her Children: An Attempt to Help Mothers to Teach Their Own Children and an Account of the Method.* Translated by Lucy E. Holland and Frances C. Turner, Swan Sonnenschein, 1898.

Piaget, Jean. *The Child's Conception of the World.* Translated by Joan and Andrew Tomlinson, Rowman & Littlefield, 2007.

———. *The Language and Thought of the Child.* Translated by Marjorie Gabain, Routledge, *2005.*

Pink, Daniel. *Whole New Mind: Why Right-Brainers Will Rule the Future.* New York: Riverhead Books, 2006.

Plotkin, Bill. *Nature and the Human Soul: Cultivating Wholeness.* Novato, CA: New World Library, 2007.

Plutarch. "On Listening to Lectures." Moralia, translated by Frank Cole Babbitt, Harvard University Press, 1927.

Porges, Stephen. *The Polyvagal Theory: Neurophysiological Foundations of Emotions, Attachment, Communication, and Self-Regulation.* New York: W. W. Norton, 2011.

Rathunde, Kevin. & Isabella, R. *Playing Music and Identity Development in Middle Adulthood: A Theoretical and Autoethnographic Account.* In R. Mantie & G.D. Smith (Eds.), *Oxford Handbook of Music Making and Leisure.* (pp. 131-149) Oxford: Oxford University Press. Published, 01/2017.

———. "Experiential Wisdom And Lifelong Learning" In J. Sinnott (Ed.), Positive Psychology and Adult Motivation (pp. 269-290). New York, Springer. Published, 2013.

———. "Creating a Context for Flow: The Importance of Personal Insight and Experience" *NAMTA,* 40*(3),* 15-27. Published, 07/01/2015.

Reindl, Verena, et al. "Brain-to-Brain Synchrony in Parent-Child Dyads and the Relationship with Emotion Regulation Revealed by fNIRS-based Hyperscanning." NeuroImage 178 (2018): 493-502.

Rizzolatti, Giacomo, and Corrado Sinigaglia. *Mirror in the Brain: How Our Minds Share Actions and Emotions.* Oxford University Press, 2016.

Robinson, Ken. *The Element: How Finding Your Passion Changes Everything.* New York: Penguin, 2009.

———. *Creative Schools: The Grassroots Revolution That's Transforming Education.* New York: Penguin, 2016.

———. *Out of Our Minds: The Power of Being Creative.* Mankato: Capstone Publishers, 2017.

Rubin, Rick. The Creative Act: A Way of Being. Penguin Press, 2023.

Ryce-Menuhin, Joel. *Jungian Sandplay: The Wonderful Therapy.* London: Routledge, 1992.

Sachs, Jonah. *Unsafe Thinking: How to Be Nimble and Bold When You Need It Most.* New York: Da Capo Lifelong Books, 2018.

Saotome, Mitsugi. *Aikido and the Harmony of Nature*. Shambhala, 1993.

Schmidt, J.A. "Flow In Education" *Northern Illinois University,* 2010 Retrieved from https://edwp.educ. msu.edu/research/wp-content/uploads/sites/10/2020/06/CHALLENGE_FlowEducation.pdf

Schrag, Peter & Diane Divoky. *The Myth of The Hyperactive Child.* New York: Dell, 1975.

Schüler, Julia, and Martin Brunner. "The Rewarding Effect of Flow Experience on Performance in a Learning Context." Psychology of Sport and Exercise, vol. 10, no. 1, 2009, pp. 1–10.

Shapiro, Shauna & White, Chris. *Mindful Discipline: A Loving Approach To Setting Limits And Raising An Emotionally Intelligent Child.* Oakland, CA: New Harbinger Publications, 2014.

Siegel, Daniel J. *The Whole-Brain Child: 12 Revolutionary Strategies to Nurture Your Child's Developing Mind.* New York: Bantam Books, 2011.

———. *The Developing Mind: How Relationships and the Brain Interact to Shape Who We Are.* 2nd ed., Guilford Press, 2012.

Shonkoff, Jack P. and others: "Place Matters. The Environments We Create Shapes the Foundations of Healthy Development" *National Scientific Council On The Development of The Child, Harvard University,* National Working Paper 16. Retrieved from www.developingchild.harvard.edu

Singer Dorothy G., Singer Jerome L. *The House of Make-Believe: Children's Play and the Developing Imagination.* Cambridge: Harvard University Press, 1990.

Stodden, David F., et al. "A Developmental Perspective on the Role of Motor Skill Competence in Physical Activity: An Emergent Relationship." Quest, vol. 60, no. 2, 2008, pp. 290–306.

Swafford, Jan. *Beethoven: Anguish and Triumph.* Houghton Mifflin Harcourt, 2014.

Taylor, Jill Bolte. *My Stroke of Insight: A Brain Scientist's Personal Journey.* New York: Penguin Books, 2009.

Taleb, Nassim Nicholas. Antifragile: Things That Gain from Disorder. New York: Random House, 2012.

Tsabary, Shefali. *The Conscious Parent: Transforming Ourselves, Empowering Our Children.* Vancouver: Namaste Publishing, 2010.

———. *Out of Control. Why Disciplining Your Child Doesn't Work and What Will.* Vancouver: Namaste Publishing, 2013.

———. *The Awakened Family: How To Raise Empowered, Resilient, and Conscious Children.* New York, Penguin Books, 2017.

Varela, Francisco J., Evan Thompson, and Eleanor Rosch. *The Embodied Mind: Cognitive Science and Human Experience.* MIT Press, 1991.

Van der Linden D, Tops M and Bakker AB (2021) The Neuroscience of the Flow State: Involvement of the Locus Coeruleus Norepinephrine System. *Frontiers in Psychology* 12:645498. doi: 10.3389/fpsyg.2021.645498

Vancil, Mark. The Last Dance. Directed by Jason Hehir, ESPN Films, Netflix, 2020.

Van Horn, Gavin, Robin Wall Kimmerer, and John Hausdoerffer, editors. Kinship: Belonging in a World of Relations. Center for Humans and Nature Press, 2021.

Vygotsky, Lev. *Mind in Society: The Development of Higher Psychological Processes*. Cambridge: Harvard University Press, 1978.

Walsh, Bari. "The Science of Resilience: Why Some Children Can Thrive Despite Adversity" *Harvard Graduate School of Education*, blog post, 2015. Retrieved from https://www.gse.harvard.edu/ideas/usable-knowledge/15/03/science-resilience

Wass, Sam V., et al. "Interpersonal Neural Entrainment During Early Social Interaction." Trends in Cognitive Sciences, vol. 24, no. 4, 2020, pp. 329–341.

Weinstein, Anne M. "Computer and Video Game Addiction—A Comparison between Game Users and Non-Game Users." The American Journal of Drug and Alcohol Abuse, vol. 36, no. 5, 2010, pp. 268–276.

Wild, Rebeca. *Raising Curious, Creative, Confident Kids: The Pestalozzi Experiment in Child-Based Education*. Boston: Shambala, 2000.

Wild, Rebeca. *Kinder im Pesta: Erfahrungen auf dem Weg zu einer vorbereiteten Umgebung für Kinder*. Arbor-Verlag, 1993.

———. *Erziehung zum Sein*. Herder, 1999.

———. *Freiheiten und Grenzen – Liebe und Respekt*. Herder, 2001.

———. *Mit Kindern leben lernen*. Herder, 2006.

Williams, Margery. *The Velveteen Rabbit*. Illustrated by William Nicholson, Doubleday, 1922.

Yogman, Michael. Garner Andrew and other pediatricians "The Power of Play. A Pediatric Role in Enhancing Development in Young Children" *Official Journal of the American Academy of Pediatrics*. Volume 142, Issue 3, September 2018 and 2025. Retrieved from https://doi.org/10.1542/peds.2018-2058

Young, Jon, Haas, Ellen & McGown Evan. *Coyote's Guide to Connecting with Nature*. Santa Cruz, CA: OWLink Media, 2010.

About the Author

CARMEN VIKTORIA GAMPER is a passionate educator, author, and lifelong explorer of the universal patterns that connect us all. A trained Montessori teacher under the guidance of Claus-Dieter Kaul, she was deeply shaped by her long-term mentors in child-guided learning, Rebeca and Mauricio Wild. She holds a Master's degree in Language and Literature, with a focus on Pedagogy.

Carmen is the founder of the New Learning Culture program, a teacher-training for flow-based educators, and co-creator of two flow-based schools in Europe. Raised bilingual in German and Italian in the Italian Alps (South Tyrol), she now writes from her home in California.

Her lifelong curiosity as a storyteller, puzzle enthusiast, and intuitive explorer has led her to advise schools worldwide, from Europe to the Huichol indigenous community in Mexico, helping to create environments that honor flow and child-guided play. Her work is dedicated to protecting the "Sacred Yes" of the human spirit. She offers online programs and resources for all who cherish children and their Inner Child, and seek to support their natural brilliance.

Continue the Journey

If this book has sparked something in you, Carmen invites you to keep going. She offers online companion programs, resources, and a growing community for parents, educators, and caregivers who want to bring Flow Learning into their daily lives.

Join the community, explore the programs, and find your own Zone at:

www.CarmenGamper.com

About the Illustrator

SYBILLE T. KRAMER is the creator of the delightful drawings in this book. She is an artist and teacher from Alto Adige/South Tyrol, Italy. She is married and she has two grown up sons, and two dogs. She discovered her love for hands-on learning materials when her children went to a Rebeca Wild based, Montessori elementary school, and after, when she homeschooled them through middle school.

Sybille turned her passion for hands-on learning into a profession and has since supported teachers and parents with the learning materials and classes she developed. She is one of driving forces of Homeschooling Italia, and also supports teachers in public schools.

https://sybilletezzelekramerartblog.wordpress.com

Flow to Learn

**A 52-Week Parent's Guide
to Recognize and Support Your Child's Flow State
—the Optimal Condition for Learning**

This uplifting, illustrated guide offers 52 weeks of practical ideas and compassionate insights to support independent play and joyful learning at home and in microschools.

Explore the 52 inspiring chapters to enrich every week of the year:

• Create activity stations that spark curiosity and learning • Discover your child's vibrant inner world, and support them through the ups and downs of childhood

• See children as guides to your own flow state to bring more fun, meaning, and purpose into your lives

*Available on Amazon,
Barnes & Noble, and
anywhere books are sold.*

The Flow Discovery Journal

Daily Questions to Spark Your Beginner's Mind.

For children ages 5 to 105

A 60-day writing, activity, and coloring journal designed to ignite curiosity and spark fresh thinking. With daily prompts for reflection, creativity, and connection, this playful book helps kids and grown-ups alike:

• Step away from screens and into meaningful discovery

• Reconnect with their own wonder and imagination

• Share joyful moments of insight with one another

Perfect for use at home, in classrooms, or in therapy sessions.

Available on Amazon,
Barnes & Noble and
anywhere books are sold.

Sample pages from the Flow Discovery Journal:

Explore the companion program,
and find your own Zone at:

www.CarmenGamper.com

Come on in!